T0243667

Crusades
and Violence

PAST IMPERFECT

See further
www.arc-humanities.org/our-series/pi

Crusades and Violence

Megan Cassidy-Welch

British Library Cataloguing in Publication Data
A catalogue record for this book is available from the British Library

ISBN (print) 9781641894753
e-ISBN (PDF) 9781802701296
e-ISBN (EPUB) 9781802701302

www.arc-humanities.org
Printed and bound in the UK (by CPI Group [UK] Ltd), USA (by Bookmasters),
and elsewhere using print-on-demand technology.

Contents

Acknowledgements

The writing of this book has been supported by an Austra-lian Research Council Discovery Project Grant on medieval histories of atrocity in warfare. It is a book that has also emerged from a longer-held interest in how we might try to understand what violence means to past societies and what controls have been created to limit it. This is a huge topic and a very short book like this one can only gesture at some of the themes, texts, and approaches that might be useful in helping us to explore a perennially difficult and contested issue. Support for thinking about the themes and methodol-ogies underpinning this book and time to write it has been gratefully received from the three universities in which I have worked whilst developing the project—Monash University, the University of Queensland, and the Australian Catholic University. There are too many people to thank by name indi-vidually here, but I extend my thanks to all those scholars, colleagues, collaborators, and friends who have helped me to shape the ideas that are sketched in this book. I want to pay particular tribute to all the librarians and archivists who have assisted me in various ways as this project has progressed. I am always so grateful to those professionals who cherish, preserve, and make available to me the manuscripts and other precious resources of the medieval past. And a special shout-out to the members of the Australian Crusade Studies Network, who workshopped this book with me and discussed lots of ways to make it better.

This book is my fourth academic book and I dedicate it to four people: Steve, Robert, and Tim, three wonderful men committed to peace, love, and knowledge, who would have been terrible crusaders. And the late Dr. Kimberley-Joy Knight, who worked as my research assistant on this project, collecting texts and images and helping me to work out what the book was really about. Kimberley died just after I secured the contract for this book so she never got to see the finished product. I hope that in its own small way, this book honours her memory. She is so very much missed and the book could not have been written without her.

Introduction

"The holy war itself was nothing more than a long act of intolerance in the name of God which is the sin against the Holy Ghost" (Runciman)

"For Christians in all ages sacred violence cannot be proposed on any grounds save that of love" (Riley-Smith)[1]

The view expressed in Stephen Runciman's above quotation—that crusading can be interpreted as a simple exercise of religious intolerance—has been significantly nuanced over the last half century. The complex religious motivations and character of the set of actions we collectively define as "crusading" has been more sensitively and carefully delineated (as Jonathan Riley-Smith's comment above indicates). Historians no longer view crusading as the undifferentiated actions of a monolithic and persecuting society. The many contexts and meanings of crusading have sparked dozens of studies on motivations for crusading, the nature and reach of crusade preaching, the environmental, cultural, liturgical, monastic, gendered, memorial, and material aspects of the crusades and the worlds that produced and responded to

---

1 Stephen Runciman, *A History of the Crusades*, 3 vols. (Cambridge: Cambridge University Press, 1951–1954), 3:480; Jonathan Riley-Smith, "Crusading as an Act of Love," *History* 65, no. 214 (1980), 177–92 at 191.

them. The "cultural turn," then, is a prominent feature of crusade scholarship over the last twenty years or so.

In this book, I intend to concentrate on medieval ideas about space, the body, emotion, and memory as ways of analyzing and understanding crusade violence. This approach will, I hope, shed new light on what is an issue of both medieval and modern concern. Violence itself was part and parcel of crusading as a military activity. But in recent times, crusade violence has also become a worryingly important element in modern medievalisms which construct the Middle Ages as a historical model for dealing with perceived present problems. The upsurge in white supremacy, racisms, and other forms of dangerous intolerance across the globe in the last decades is all too frequently accompanied by images and assumptions about the violence of crusading as something to be honoured and replicated. It is my hope that by parsing more carefully how cultures construct and remember violence will help us to understand better how and why this has occurred.

How, then, should we now understand the innate violence of crusading? In modern popular and political cultures, it is still assumed that the explanation "God wills it" (*Deus vult*, in the medieval Latin) both sufficed to justify all crusading action and obviated the need for any individual or collective reflection on crusading violence. There also remains the tendency to assume that the logic of crusading violence can be explained principally as a matter of religious philosophy and law. Just war theory, which laid out the rationale for just and (less explicitly) holy warfare, remains a dominant explicatory paradigm for imagining how the actions of crusaders were guided until laws of war came to be more codified from the thirteenth century onward. But given that just/holy war theory at this time was principally concerned with the justifications for going to war rather than the conduct of war itself, it is a little too easy to imagine those who participated in crusading were not concerned about the nature and extent of the violence they conducted in these holy wars, nor reflected on what we might call the ethics of violence.

But was this the case? This book suggests that we shift our gaze from viewing the violence embedded in the act of crusading as entirely a matter of theology and/or intellectual history, to consider crusading violence socially and culturally. By this I mean that we take seriously the insights offered by the spatial turn, the emotional turn, the history of the body, the turn to memory, the material turn, and so on.[2] Medievalists may well be reading these words thinking "but we already do this." Yet in relation to the question of violence during the crusades, there is work to be done to bridge the excellent scholarship that is already being done and the lingering perception of crusade violence as either typically medieval and thoughtless, or as a matter principally for canonists and theologians and somehow removed from the actions of individuals who committed it. Including what we might call "the cultural turn" in crusade studies in discussions of the nature and meaning of crusading violence offers new insights into the practice of violence, the place of violence, and the concerns about violence that underpinned crusading activity.

In recent decades, a burgeoning scholarship on medieval violence has asked us to think much more contextually about how violence operates in past societies and why. This book builds on that scholarship and also makes a plea for the conversation to move away once and for all from futile quests to determine historical hierarchies of violence (was it better or worse than in modern times?, was crusading violence more or less brutal than "normal" medieval violence?). These sorts of questions invite only historical disdain for past peoples who

---

2 For some useful introductions and overviews, see for example: Riccardo Bavaj et al., *Doing Spatial History* (London: Routledge, 2022); Jan Plamper, *The History of Emotions: An Introduction*, trans. Keith Tribe (Oxford: Oxford University Press, 2015); Willemijn Ruberg, *History of the Body* (London: Bloomsbury, 2020); Geoffrey Cubitt, *History and Memory* (Manchester: Manchester University Press, 2007); Leonora Auslander et al., "AHR Conversation: Historians and the Study of Material Culture," *American Historical Review* 114 (2009): 1354–1404.

thought and acted in ways that we do not easily recognize. It is important, I argue here, to understand the place of violence and its meaning in societies. This does not mean that we fall into moral relativism and accept historical violence without question, judgement, or even outrage. But the questions we ask about how people thought and acted in the past and the scholarly judgements we make about those thoughts and actions, need to be based both on the historical evidence that exists and the ever more informative historiographical, theoretical, and methodological tools we bring to interpret and understand that evidence.

In this book, I trace stories of crusading violence across the twelfth and thirteenth centuries. This is a fairly conventional framework for defining "the crusading period"; crusading and crusading language lingered far longer than that. But for the purposes of this book it is a manageable framework that captures some significant continuities and changes in crusading activity across time. From the preaching of what came to be known by modern historians as the First Crusade (preached by Pope Urban II at Clermont in 1095) to the aftermath of the fall of the city of Acre to the Mamluks in 1291, crusading encompassed campaigns to the Middle East, the Baltic and northeastern Europe, the south of France, the Iberian peninsula, North Africa, and beyond; campaigns against individuals and groups; prayer and liturgical activities including on the "home front"; diversity of participants and victims (in terms of gender, race, class); the shaping and reshaping of language to describe what "crusading" actually was; the shifting fortunes of crusade targets, particularly the city of Jerusalem. There are many other items one could add to this list and I do not claim to be covering all of these. Nonetheless, this period of historical time reflects the inception and development of crusading thought and practice so remains a useful window through which to direct our gaze.

What constitutes a crusade gathered a large scholarship in the mid to late twentieth century when various schools of thought arose. One of these asserted the central place of Jerusalem as the destination or target of a crusade (the "traditionalist" view); another asserted that crusades were penitential wars fought against any enemy that gained the reward of an indulgence to its participants (the "pluralist" view); a third focussed on the place of popular and personal religious enthusiasm, particularly eschatological dimensions in defining a crusade (the "popularist" view); while a fourth took a broad view that a crusade was any holy war authorized by God (the "generalist" view). There are more sophisticated debates attached to all of these categories but a common preoccupation was how to define a phenomenon that did not have a single word to describe it until the thirteenth century. In recent times, interest in the issue of definition has significantly diminished as scholars increasingly look to contextualize and acknowledge the great variety of ways in which the crusade was understood, promoted, and experienced. For the purposes of this book, I am using the category of "crusade" to discuss holy wars in a variety of locations that attracted remission (forgiveness) of sins.

Just and Holy War and Its Interpretive Limitations

Violence in warfare was partly governed by the broad theory of just war, which deals both with the conditions in which it is just to go to war (the principle of *ius ad bellum*) and the question of just conduct during war (the principle of *ius in bello*). The first of these conditions include three inherent requirements of just cause, proper authority, and right intention. The scholarship on just war theory is voluminous, but it is standard to locate its early expression by Augustine of Hippo, its "revival" and reimagining by the canonists and theologians of the eleventh and twelfth centuries, and its more schematic application from the mid-thirteenth century onwards and the formal codification of the laws of war as a part of the rise of the modern sovereign state. Just war theory itself was thus not fixed or static throughout the medieval period and the example of the crusades illustrates quite well its dynamism. Crusades were distinctive in that they brought together ideas of penance, pilgrimage, and the promise of eternal reward (the remission of sins) with just war theory to create a new sort of "holy war." Foundational to the idea of crusades as holy wars was God's authority, the most legitimate authority of all, which was exercised through God's representative on earth, the Pope.

Ideas relating to just war prior to Augustine are biblical (for instance, Exodus 32:26–28), classical (for example Plato's *Republic* considers war as an ethical problem, while Cicero's *On Duties* noted that wars are just if they recover goods and/or punish or repel enemies), and legal. Augustine's own comments on just war were also fairly unsystematic, with elements of what would later be drawn together as a "theory" of just and holy war scattered across a number of different texts. His *Letter to Vincentius* (408) stressed the causes of "good" war and the notion of eternal warfare and noted that the punishment of heretics was a sort of *caritas*, or act of Christian love; his *City of God* (completed by 426) argued that violence could be benevolent. Augustine also considered what constituted illegitimate motivation for warfare—the "desire to harm, cruelty of punishment, implacable intent, severity or rebellion, the desire for domination, these are what are culpable in war" (*Contra Faustum Manicheum*, book 22, §74, ca. 383), an idea that was echoed by later Christian writers such as Isidore of Seville in his *Etymologiae* (compiled from before 620 until Isidore's death in 636).

A few elements of Augustine's thinking were particularly influential for later crusade commentators. First was the idea that individual motivations and virtue are key to whether war is just. Second was the idea that "just wars avenge injuries." These points situated individual right intent and legitimate purpose at the centre of the motivation to engage in just war. At the same time, Augustine confronted head-on the question of virtuous killing:

> There are some whose killing God orders, either by a law, or by an express command to a particular person at a particular time. In fact, one who owes a duty of obedience to

the giver of the command does not himself "kill"—he is an instrument, a sword in its user's hand. For this reason, the commandment forbidding killing was not broken by those who have waged wars on the authority of God (*City of God*, book 1, §21).[3]

This point emphasized legitimate authority to call for (God's orders), and the sanctification of violence in God's name. It also absolved the individual from any accusation of homicide as the soldier in these sorts of wars is an "instrument" of God's will.

The revival of interest in just war theory from the eleventh century has been well documented as arising from a range of more immediate historical factors. These include a Church increasingly keen to limit and direct knightly violence, the development of intellectual cultures and institutions supporting both the revival of Roman law and its compilation, and a reformist papacy keen to intervene more directly in the pastoral affairs of all Christians. In terms of just war theory, medieval canonists such as Gratian and his later twelfth-century commentators showed new interest in just war. In *Causa* 23 of his compilation of canon law known as the *Decretum* (ca. 1140), Gratian addressed among other topics the moral dangers inherent in knightly violence, what legitimate authority exists for calling for war, and the sorts of injuries that war might legitimately avenge. Gratian was clear that the Church constituted a legitimate authority to wage war and that war could justly be waged against heretics and heathens. He did not specifically address the crusades (although the *Decretum* was compiled some decades after the "success" of the First Crusade). The later twelfth-century/early thirteenth-century glosses on the *Decretum* and other papal letters laid out more schematically the criteria for just war, as did several thirteenth-century theologians. Thomas Aquinas (d. 1274) described the three principal criteria for waging a just war (legitimate authority, just cause, right intention) in his *Summa*

---

3 From Augustine, *City of God*, trans. G. Evans (London: Penguin, 2003).

Theologiae; the *Summa de penitentia* of the Dominican canonist Raymond de Penyafort (d. 1275) laid out five criteria for waging war; and Henry of Segusio (or "Hostiensis," d. 1271) mapped seven types of just and unjust war, which included war against infidels. Augustine continued to be invoked in all these iterations of just war "theory."

The regulation of violence was part of the Peace of God and Truce of God movements emerging mostly during the eleventh century. These "movements"—ecclesiastical attempts to harness and limit knightly violence—also included elements of protection for civilians. The sort of violence that the Church wished to regulate at this time was principally the violence committed by a knighthood interested in asserting or protecting property. But the intervention of ecclesiastical authorities in the conduct of violence provided the idea that war could be a matter for legitimate ecclesiastical intervention and the idea that conduct in warfare should be limited. Clergy and women, for instance, were supposed to be protected, while the conduct of knightly violence was limited (ideally if not in reality) to certain days of the week. The control of violence in the Peace and Truce of God movements did not condemn violence entirely; in fact, one striking and unusual situation was cited by Andrew of Fleury who reported that in 1038 the archbishop of Bourges used military force to enforce the Peace of God in his diocese.[4] These sorts of ideas were circulating at the same time as the revival of just/holy war theory in medieval western legal cultures.

Even this superficial sketch of just war theory reveals that the conversation was "live" about the legitimacy of engaging in war during the period of the crusades. But it also reveals that much of the "theory" around just war focussed on *ius ad bello* rather than *ius in bello*. This might simply be because the divisions between the two categories were not neatly imagined in reality. But perhaps the established "canon" of

---

4 Thomas Head, "Andrew of Fleury and the Peace League of Bourges," *Historical Reflections/Réflexions historiques* 14, no. 3 (1987): 513–29.

just war theorists is not as inclusive of ideas as it might be. Much commentary on just/holy war theory only includes the voices of the theologians, philosophers, canonists, lawyers— lettered men of the Catholic tradition—who wrote those compendia and collections that have gathered historical authority. It might seem that there is not much evidence to show that medieval people worried about or debated "right behaviours" in combat if we focus solely on the words of these medieval theorists.

I suggest that perhaps we have not yet cast our nets widely enough on this topic, and that what we understand of medieval attitudes to acceptable and unacceptable conduct is to be found in sources other than purely philosophical and jurisprudential ones. Reading beyond the usual commentators, we discover that crusaders did indeed think about and discuss how and why violence was putatively legitimate in war, and what violence signified and reflected. These questions and ideas were intimately connected to broader cultural and social contexts and their constitutive vocabularies. To delve into these contexts means thinking about place, the body, emotion, memory, and many other seemingly nebulous or unconnected ideas that frame violence. Doing so helps us to see how medieval crusaders determined the nature and meaning of violence in a range of historical settings.

Medieval Violence, Crusading Violence

What was medieval violence? In a fairly recent book, Warren Brown delineated the various forms of violence that we find throughout the Middle Ages and the various social and cultural norms that informed them. Brown emphasized the public and instrumental function of violence in many medieval contexts including war, justice, honour, politics, ritual, and so on, arguing that the violence exercised by individuals— what we might call "private" violence—remained a useful social tool even as authorities (such as kings) increasingly claimed the right to regulate violence themselves. Brown's work emphasized violence as power, both for individuals who used violence to assert their rights, for instance, and for institutions that aimed to order society. He noted that even the Latin words for violence were various (and tended to be expressed quite specifically by terms such as *occidere* (to kill), *pugnare* (to fight) and *vulnere* (to wound), rather than by the umbrella term *violentia* which denoted "vehemence, impetuosity, or ferocity."[5] Thus, to understand violence—both what it was and what it meant—is an historical issue. In what follows, violence is approached as a set of both interpersonal and discursive actions intended to express and enforce a desired outcome. In war, such actions mostly involve physical hurt and although the scale of this might differ from the sort of interpersonal violence experienced in a non-war setting, the instruments of physical violence (e.g., a sword) might be the same.

A prodigious historiography has explored the logic of medieval violence in a number of different contexts, together broadly reinforcing the point I make here, which is that it is not possible to separate acts of violence from the cultural, social, and political environments from which they emerge. David Nirenberg's studies of medieval anti-Judaism are one excellent example of how "everyday" violence against medieval Jewish communities—mocking, stone throwing, ritualized anger—created the specific social background of normalized violence which then allowed for episodes of "cataclysmic violence" to occur, such as the massacres committed during the Shepherds' Crusade of 1320. Other historians have considered knightly cultures as forging and legitimizing the performance of masculine violence which was such a prominent part of crusading. Richard Kaeuper's many studies of the culture of medieval chivalry have used the evidence of romance literature to show that chivalry did not necessarily act as a behavioural restraint against violence, but was a force that could both reinforce and complicate social and political order. The warrior class of medieval Europe performed a violence

---

5 Warren C. Brown, *Violence in Medieval Europe* (London: Routledge, 2011), 7.

that both asserted hegemonic military masculinity and made such a masculinity troublesome for the royal governments that tried to accommodate and contain it.[6]

A large literature also exists on urban violence, including most recently Hannah Skoda's work analyzing the communicative function of interpersonal violence in northern France during the late thirteenth and early fourteenth centuries. The social and legal norms around the exercise and censure of violence have been explored by scholars such as Claude Gauvard, while Pieter Spierenburg's studies on homicide rates and meanings of interpersonal violence through (inter alia) the explanatory frames of "the civilizing process" and the modern state's monopoly of violence. Daniel Smail has shown that medieval violence operated as a form of power and method of lordship, arguing that although older historiographies privilege violence as the main area of concern in premodern governments (by asserting either that the state is an "agent of civilization" that moderates interpersonal violence or is an "agent of domination" that mobilizes violence in its service), evidence from medieval courts of law shows more concern with debt than interpersonal violence. Indeed, Smail argues that "courts practiced their violence more often on debtors and especially on goods and things" and that this, not the regulation of bodily violence, is perhaps the more significant foundation of modern statism.[7]

---

6 David Nirenberg, *Communities of Violence: Persecution of Minorities in the Middle Ages* (Princeton: Princeton University Press, 1996); Nirenberg, *Anti Judaism: The Western Tradition* (New York: Norton, 2013); Richard Kaeuper, *Holy Warriors: the Religious Ideology of Chivalry* (Philadelphia: University of Pennsylvania Press, 2009).

7 Hannah Skoda, *Medieval Violence: Physical Brutality in Northern France, 1270-1330* (Oxford: Oxford University Press, 2013); Claude Gauvard, *Violence et ordre public au Moyen âge* (Paris: Picard, 2005); Pieter Spierenberg, *Violence and Punishment: Civilising the Body Through Time* (Cambridge: Polity, 2013) ; Daniel Smail, *The Consumption of Justice: Emotions, Publicity, and Legal Culture in Marseille, 1264-1423* (Ithaca: Cornell University Press, 2003).

Most recently, historians of medieval religious violence have increasingly taken a long view of the historical relationship between the nature of war and the Church. Jean Flori has argued that the politicization of religion is one reason why violence became embedded in Christian thought and practice in late antiquity and the early Middle Ages. This was elaborated upon by medieval reformist popes who progressively sacralized warfare in the period prior to the crusades. Thomas Sizgorich's exploration of violence in late antiquity outlined a form of "militant piety" common to early Islam and Christianity that constructed the identities of both. An influential study by Philippe Buc explored how ideas of violent purification that developed alongside apocalyptic ideas became dominant in western Christian thought. Buc thought that Christian monotheism's "historical semantics account for quite idiosyncratic forms of violence. It provided the matrix for holy war, martyrdom, and terror, and imprinted itself on successive manifestations of violence." Religious violence, then, is understood as a problem of theology that had a profound impact on social behaviour across a long sweep of historical time, not just the Middle Ages.[8]

Yet how soldiers themselves understood violence and its limits in war has been explored almost entirely as a matter of modern military history. A huge literature on conduct in modern warfare agrees that although violence is the essence of war, some acts of violence committed during war are considered to exceed the normal violence of combat and conflict (such as massacres, the murder of non-combatants, rape, and the deliberate displacement of people). Contemporary societies call such acts "atrocities," usually described in legal and moral categories under the overall term "war crimes."

---

8 Jean Flori, *Guerre sainte, jihad, croisade: Violence et religion dans le christianisme et l'islam* (Paris: Aubier, 2001); Thomas Sizgorich, *Violence and Belief in Late Antiquity: Militant Devotion in Christianity and Islam* (Philadelphia: University of Pennsylvania Press, 2009); Philippe Buc, *Holy War, Martyrdom, and Terror: Christianity, Violence, and the West* (Philadelphia: University of Pennsylvania Press, 2015).

Efforts to prosecute those who commit atrocity in war are mostly specific to modern international law, which emphasizes both criminality and fundamental moral collapse—what Hannah Arendt called "radical," "extreme," or "thought-defying" evil—as the markers of atrocity. Although historians and others have mostly moved away from Arendt's category of "evil" as a way to explain atrocity in order to argue that such violence possesses its own internal, rational logic, the literature on modern wartime atrocity frames its central questions as essentially moral—why do people choose to commit atrocities in war?—and legal—how can we prevent atrocities from happening again, using the mechanisms of international law and human rights?

These are paradigms borrowed by some medievalists to consider the longer history of acceptable and unacceptable violence in medieval war. Some have made efforts to interpret medieval war violence through the lens of genocide studies, arguing that ethnic differences and (proto) nation-building efforts from the eleventh century saw the development of an ideology of mass killing in which medieval people were encouraged to think "genocidally."[9] The period of the crusades, perceived by some as an ethnic confrontation, has even been framed as a set of extermination events that "ushered genocide into the west."[10] Such histories follow a well-rehearsed story of increasing exclusion and persecution throughout the Middle Ages on the basis of ethnicity and difference, while also implicitly reinforcing old stereotypes of the Middle Ages as endemically cruel and even entrapped by Catholic barbarity.

There is no doubt that crusading was violent, often appallingly so, and that religious and ethnic difference was a motivation for violence. But crusading was above all a set

---

9 Len Scales, "Central and Late Medieval Europe" in *The Oxford Handbook of Genocide Studies*, ed. D. Bloxham and D. Moses (Oxford: Oxford University Press, 2013), 280–303.

10 Mark Pegg, *A Most Holy War: the Albigensian Crusade and the Battle for Christendom* (Oxford: Oxford University Press, 2008).

of religious movements motivated by a complex set of pious motives that cannot be adequately described as "genocidal." We need to take seriously that, as a military *and* religious phenomenon, crusading emerged from and was informed by specific cultural and social environments, including the knightly cultures of western Europe, preaching cultures, the monastic cultures which inscribed its memory, and so on. As Marcus Bull wrote: "For crusaders, then, the question of why they were going on crusade could not meaningfully be separated from consideration of the resources that were available in their world—emotional, economic, social, political—to turn idea into action."[11] I would add that the question of why violence was enacted and the degrees to which it was questioned requires the same highly specific contextual sensitivity.

Was crusading violence distinctive and different from any other sort of medieval violence? Susannah Throop has recently explored this question in a significant chapter in the *Cambridge World History of Violence*. Arguing that it is important to understand crusading as part of medieval culture and not separate from it, Throop argues that crusading violence is distinctive because it was "spiritually beneficial for the individual and the Christian community, was directed at the 'enemies of Christ,' and took the form of organized and purportedly organized endeavours."[12] Throop rightly notes that crusading violence is not particularly distinctive in its practices or even its broad conceptual framework (such as just/holy war theory), given that many other military activ-

11 Marcus Bull, "Muslims and Jerusalem in Miracle Stories c. 1000-c.1200: Reflections on the Study of First Crusaders' Motivations," in *The Experience of Crusading, Volume 1: Western Approaches*, ed. Marcus Bull and Norman Housley (Cambridge: Cambridge University Press, 2001), 13–38 at 37.

12 Susannah Throop, "Not Cruelty but Piety: Circumscribing European Crusading Violence," in *The Cambridge World History of Violence, Volume 2: AD500-1500*, edited by Matthew Gordon, Richard W. Kaeuper, and Harriet Zurndorfer (Cambridge: Cambridge University Press, 2020), 411–25 at 413.

ities used similar techniques and rhetoric. Nor does papal authorization make crusading violence distinctive, as some violence that occurred during the crusades was not authorized. Rather, argues Throop, crusader violence is distinctive because piety and spiritual benefit were at its heart. These are useful points with which to proceed in this book. They help us to make central questions about individual and collective decision-making in war, and they help us to think carefully about what violence was meant to signify and achieve in the cultures that produced it. I argue here that crusade violence shared many aspects with violence committed in other medieval contexts—it was justified by ideas of justice, honour, correction, and legitimacy, for a start—but the combination of individual spiritual benefit through collective military action was something different. And it is by better understanding the cultural forces that shaped these aspects of crusading that its violence can be explained.

Crusade thought or ideology was not laid out at the Council of Clermont in 1095 and set in stone thereafter. What we know of what Pope Urban II said at that famous Council is entirely located in subsequent narrative reports, themselves increasingly concerned to shape a set of events and ideas that was continually unfolding. What crusading meant for individuals and groups, what it was supposed to achieve, and how it was practised, evolved and shifted across time. As a dynamic set of structures just as much as a set of events, crusading responded to different conditions and directions. It is therefore important to grapple with a variety of crusading sources and their many complexities, including textual histories and borrowings; questions about reception and imagined audiences; the nature of eye-witnessing; and the motives behind the production of texts. Crusaders learned about violence and shared that knowledge through many networks emanating from schools, courts, preachers, singers, families, objects, and things. Personal writings such as letters, texts that were meant to connect crusaders from particular regions in specific conflicts, official histories that were commissioned and circulated for dissemination in organized communities, shared experience in liturgies that connected ideas and people, armies that mustered behind family or dynastic insignia and were sometimes informed by military ordinances, attendance at sermons that preached the crusade (which was made mandatory in 1234 by Pope Gregory IX)—these were all means by which ideas about crusading and violence were transmitted and reworked.

Overall then, this book argues that although just/holy war theory remains of value in helping us to understand how and why the limits of war were articulated in some medieval intellectual and clerical circles, it is in texts that try to make sense of events, communicate the importance of religious warfare, stimulate remembrance and future action, and communicate personal experiences at war, that we can uncover how medieval people debated and wrestled with the idea and practice of violence and its limits. Simply put, crusading was not thought by its participants to be an opportunity for a violent free for all just because it came with divine authority and the apparatus of just/holy war theory.

Conclusion

In tackling this topic and taking this approach, I want to offer something to scholars, students, and others interested in this topic that asks us to think carefully about where violence comes from and how it is justified or condemned. I hope to show that the medieval contexts that informed the practices of religious violence were many. I attempt to bring together a range of scholarly perspectives on crusades and violence, not to synthesize historiographies necessarily but to lay out (to some degree) the very many dimensions of thinking about violence and holy war that have informed this book. In so doing, I take issue with the racist glorification of crusading violence by the far right in recent times. As many medievalists know, it is difficult to see the complex, nuanced, interactive, and differentiated past that we call "the Middle Ages" being brought into the service of hatred and modern violence as some sort of justification. The appropriation of crusading rhetoric and symbols by some extremists is founded on the fabrication of a past that did not exist, as well as the desire to attempt to legitimize repugnant acts of violence by linking them to the imagined precedent of dichotomous histories. There is no doubt that hateful violence was innate to the crusade in various ways. But as this book hopes to show, medieval people, including crusaders, were much more thoughtful about their actions and the world in which they lived than is sometimes understood—even in the conduct of violence.

I am also critiquing the weight placed on the notion of the decline of violence in larger historical narratives. There is much nuanced work on medieval violence (the handful of authors I have mentioned above are only a few of dozens), and on modern violence. Yet the grand progressivist narrative that seeks to situate modernity as something of an antidote to the barbarity of the Middle Ages is still one that dominates much popular and some academic discourse around the nature of historical violence. This book will not make arguments about whether the violence in the Middle Ages was more or less, better or worse than violence today, as such arguments are, to my mind, not very useful if we want to really think about how violence emanates from and informs societies and cultures. This book takes the position that to historicize war violence is not to prop up a view of the Middle Ages as more violent than other ages or even to enter into that tired debate. It is to seek to understand how cultures and societies draw lines around the conduct of war, and how we as historians should walk those lines.

There are necessarily a number of caveats that need to be made about what this book can cover. Readers should note that crusading took place over a long period of time in many different locations. What was true for thinking about one crusade might not be true for another. I am a historian of the European west, so this is where my main source base and attention will focus. I will attempt to bring in other perspectives where I can, but my focus will remain on my area of expertise which is the western/crusader viewpoint. This itself is complex. But I want to make clear that other perspectives on this large topic are just as important. Given the limited citations in this book, I will only refer to translations of the primary source material where available. At times, I stick very close to the primary texts, and I hope that the non-specialist reader will bear with me as I do so; the approach I am taking here sometimes requires digging deep into the words and images that medieval people used to talk about bigger issues.

Chapter 1

Spaces of Violence

Crusading was an inherently spatial practice, involving mobility (physical and imagined), claims to possession of territory, settlement, and the transformation of cities and landscapes. At the very heart of crusading lay the connection between crusade and the spiritual journey of pilgrimage. This remained strong throughout the twelfth and thirteenth centuries even as crusade destinations moved well beyond the Holy Land. Both crusade and pilgrimage were penitential activities undertaken for spiritual benefit, both involved a vow or oath, and both were undertakings premised on the idea and reality of travel. Famously described by Jonathan Riley-Smith as like a "military monastery on the move," the crusade was described in Latin sources in spatial terms such as *iter Sancti Sepulchri* (journey to the Holy Sepulchre), *via* (way, path), *profectio* (journey), while crusaders were *peregrini* (pilgrims), as well as *crucesignati* (those signed with the cross), and *milites Christi* (knights of Christ).

Given crusading's links to ideas about place and practices of movement, space provides a useful interpretive lens through which to explore crusade violence. This is partly because the military reality of a crusade was always underpinned by purposeful ideas about its destination. To look more closely at the spatial hermeneutics of crusading is to gain insight into how certain locations became sites of violence, how violence was practised to assert territorial ownership, and how violence worked to sacralize places. Thinking about these questions also helps us to situate crusading in the broader socio-cultural contexts that informed and legitimized it. As I noted in the previous chapter, Philippe Buc and Susannah Throop have recently argued that the history of the crusades is part of a longer and deeper story about Christian violence. I would add that theory and method play a role in telling this story, too. Here, what some have called the "spatial turn" in history is helpful in guiding us through some of the rhetoric around the performance and legitimization of violence, and the many discursive contexts that shaped it.

Henri Lefebvre imagined that an overlapping "spatial triad"—physical space, social space, and mental space—is a useful way to describe the production of space. These are useful schema with which to think about historical violence, too: the locations of violence, the social delineations marked out by and performed by violence, and the imaginaries of violence (metaphorical, rhetorical, and so on) remind us that violence as a social behaviour involves action and expression, performance and meaning, interactions and ideologies.[1] Lefebvre also thought that violence itself is a form of spatial production. That is, the practice and impact of violence creates territory, not only in the sense of bordered location or proprietary ownership but also in practices of segmentation and separation. Likewise, the geographer Doreen Massey thought that places are created from articulations of difference, writing that "space [is] full of power and symbolism, a complex web of relations of domination and subordination, of solidarity and cooperation."[2] Divisions, power relations, collective actions are also practices of violence which can be mapped historically.

If we look at the particular example of crusading, spatial thinking and its connection with practices of violence is also

---

1 Henri Lefebvre, *The Production of Space*, trans. D. Nicholson Smith (Oxford: Blackwell, 1974).

2 Doreen Massey, "Politics and Space/Time," in *Place and the Politics of Identity*, ed. M. Keith and S. Pile (London: Routledge, 1993), 141–61 at 156.

evident. I consider here four specific examples of crusading violence and its representation in order to explore how justifications for military action were tied to cultural understandings of liberation, purification, vengeance, ownership, and possession of Christian property, and to illustrate some of the connections between space and violence. I dig into some specific texts here, too, to show how important it is to understand the microdetail before making big claims about violence and history.

Mobilizing Gender

The feminization of places is a feature of crusading rhetoric, especially in relation to Jerusalem and Constantinople, two cities fundamental to the crusading movement. Jerusalem was, of course, the actual and avowed destination of many crusades, and the central motif for much crusade preaching. The Christian city of Constantinople was part of the First Crusade's journey, the scene of the Fourth Crusade, and a city that represented the division of the Latin west and the Greek east. For popes like Urban II and Innocent III, it was hoped that this division might be eradicated through the common Christian act of crusading. Both Jerusalem and Constantinople also witnessed some of crusading's most notorious scenes of violence, Jerusalem in 1099 when it was invaded by the crusading armies, and Constantinople in 1204 when it was captured and looted during the Fourth Crusade.

The representation of the cities in crusading texts composed prior to and after these violent events tells us much about the layers of rhetoric and imagery that built justifications and meanings of violence. In the cases of Jerusalem and Constantinople, the biblical genealogy on which feminized representations were based helped to blur temporal distinctions between Christian pasts and the present. This also invited reflection on violence as a constitutive element of crusading, linking it to familial duty, liberation, vengeance for dishonour, and purification. Although there existed a spatial gendering of cities independent of crusade or biblical discourses (Tyche, the city goddess, was understood to oversee the fortune of cities, for instance), the gendered language of place worked effectively in crusade texts to help build a vocabulary of violence.

This was especially true of Jerusalem. Many crusade preachers and commentators found the image of Jerusalem as woman to be a useful characterization and sermons and chronicles contain reference to biblical verses which speak of the city of Jerusalem as a wife, a mother, a grieving widow, or a despoiled bride. The Lamentations of Jeremiah, a reflection on the destruction of the city by the Babylonians, personified the city as widow, as the daughter of Sion, as a woman made unclean by menstruation (Lamentations 1:1–2; 1:17); Ezekiel 16 represented Jerusalem as a fallen woman to be chastised for fornication and faithlessness; Ezekiel 23 represented Jerusalem as a prostitute and defiled woman whose wickedness would end with judgement and punishment; Revelations 21:2 gendered Jerusalem feminine, too, talking of the city as a beautiful woman; and Galatians 4:25 described Jerusalem as a mother. Post-biblical thought also gendered the city feminine—Augustine represented Jerusalem, the Church, as a slave-woman (*ancilla*) and a mother in his famous rendering of the two cities, where the earthly city (founded on the love of the self) was oppressed by greed and pride and governed by the devil, while the City of God was a place of harmonious and collective glorification of God. The identification of the two cities with real cities was a post-Augustinian development which became newly invigorated during the period of the crusades.[3]

Such imagery resonated (albeit not uniformly) with the Latin chroniclers and crusade propagandists of the early twelfth century, some of whom represented the city of Jerusalem as distressed and begging to be liberated by the Franks, according to the Benedictine Robert of Reims. For Fulcher of Chartres, "justly is Jerusalem like a mother who rejoices over her daughter Tyre at whose right hand she sits crowned

---

3 Sylvia Schein, *Gateway to the Heavenly City: Crusader Jerusalem and the Catholic West (1099–1187)* (London: Routledge, 2006).

as befits her rank," while Baudri of Bourgeuil mourned that Jerusalem had been "deprived of her own children, led off into captivity, suffering so many historical upheavals until the coming of the Saviour." The Norman author of the *Gesta Tancredi*, Ralph of Caen, told of crusaders in 1099 rushing to Jerusalem and kissing the walls of the city "as if to embrace their wives."[4] There are layers of complexity in all these representations that this book cannot fully address. But broadly, the image of the city of Jerusalem as woman conformed with biblical tropes and schema while also providing a neat way for chroniclers of the First Crusade to describe the nature of the holy war itself as a liberating act of religious duty.

As the reward for crusading (remission of sins) came to be extended to non-combatants from the time of Pope Innocent III (r. 1198–1216), the imagery used to motivate participation (including individual prayer, collective liturgy, financial support) came to appeal to a wider audience than those engaged in military activity. Gendered imagery of the polluted and grieving Jerusalem continued to be used, even as the actual locations of crusading diversified over the course of the thirteenth century. An example of this is Pope Innocent III's 1198 letter, *Plorans ploravit*, which was addressed to the bishop of Syracuse and the Cistercian abbot Lucas of Sambucina, entrusting them with preaching the Fourth Crusade in Sicily; this letter was one of the first direct actions on behalf of the Holy Land undertaken by Innocent after his consecration in 1198. The letter opens with the image of the Old Testament matriarch Rachel mourning her children, the sons of Israel (from Matthew 2:17–18 echoing Jeremiah 31:15): "Weeping the Church weeps and a voice is heard in Rama of weeping and great lamentation." The letter describes the terrible acts

---

4 Fulcher of Chartres, A History of the Expedition to Jerusalem, 1095–1127, trans. F. R. Ryan (Knoxville: University of Tennessee Press, 1969), 238; The Historia Ierosolimitana of Baldric of Bourgeuil, ed. Steven Biddlecombe (Woodbridge: Boydell, 2014), 1–95; The Gesta Tancredi of Ralph of Caen: A History of the Normans on the First Crusade, ed. D. S. and B. S. Bachrach (Farnham: Ashgate, 2005), 138.

of sacrilege and violence that had been visited on the Holy Land, narrating almost verbatim Psalm 78: "The heathens are come into the Lord's inheritance, they have attacked his temple, they have made Jerusalem as a place to keep fruit, they have given the dead bodies of thy servants to be meat for the fowls of the air: the flesh of the saints for the beasts of the earth. They have poured out their blood as water, round about Jerusalem and there was none to bury them."[5] Similar imagery is found in Pope Gregory IX's 1234 bull, *Rachel suum videns*, which also presented mother church as Rachel weeping over her slaughtered children: "we ought to lament when...the city of the great king...which the son of God consecrated with his own blood...is now enslaved." The same bull said that Jerusalem has been soiled, "as if polluted by menstrual blood"; this pollution imagery was meant to equate the travesties done to Jerusalem ("abominations and filthiness") with the despoilment of both the female city and the mother Church, which in Pope Gregory's view has been violated and occupied by "a shameful throng of the most unclean people."[6]

The female gendering of Jerusalem also formed part of the vocabulary of legitimate violence that took place in the city. We can see this in representations of the massacre that took place once the crusaders entered Jerusalem in 1099. The city had been besieged for five weeks and, for western commentators, its eventual capture was thought to have restored the city to its previous dignity. This act of "restoration" involved, according to the anonymous author of the *Gesta Francorum*, crusaders wading up to their ankles in the blood of the massacred local populace.[7] This is an image that

---

5 Innocent III, "Regesta sive epistolae," in *Opera omnia*, vol. 1, Patrologia Latina 214 (Paris: Migne, 1890), no. 302, col. 263–66.

6 *Rachel suum videns*, in Jessalynn Bird, Edward Peters and James M. Powell, eds., *Crusade and Christendom: Annotated Documents in Translation from Innocent III to the Fall of Acre, 1187–1291* (Philadelphia: University of Pennsylvania Press, 2013), 269–76 at 271.

7 *Gesta Francorum et aliorum Hierosolymitanorum*, ed. Rosalind T. Hill (Oxford: Oxford University Press, 1972), 91–92.

was subsequently repeated by many medieval writers and although this was not the first massacre that had taken place during the long journey of the various crusading armies to the Holy Land in the period 1095-1099 as I will outline in the next chapter, it is nonetheless a moment that has acquired unique valency in the history of crusading violence. Historians have explained the massacre in various ways: as part of a longer story of Christian apocalypticism that justified violence, as a bloodbath that was deliberately exaggerated to underscore the importance of Jerusalem itself, as an episode that was represented to emphasize the righteous anger and retributive justice that were central elements of holy war.[8]

The details of the massacre vary according to the sources. Benjamin Kedar usefully mapped these, showing that some twelfth-century Latin reports emphasized the cleansing and punitive nature of the bloodshed—Raymond of Aguilers, for example, opined that it was "justice that the Temple of Solomon should receive the blood of the pagans who blasphemed God there for many years"—while others reported that no mercy was shown to those Muslims who were begging for their lives.[9] Bartolf of Nangis thought that showing no mercy reminded crusaders of the fate of King Saul who showed mercy to Agag, angering God; Albert of Aachen, who used similarly graphic language to describe the 1096 massacre of Jews in the Rhineland, thought that three massacres occurred on three days and that even crying women and children were shown no mercy. These acts of violence were justified by medieval chroniclers and others as performing what Penny Cole called "a comprehensive rite of purification."[10] Later in the twelfth century, archbishop Wil-

---

8 Benjamin Kedar, "The Jerusalem Massacre of July 1099 in the Western Historiography of the Crusades," *Crusades* 3 (2004): 15-75.

9 *Le "Liber" de Raymond d'Aguilers*, ed. L. L. Hill and J. R. Hill (Paris: Geuthner, 1969), 150-51.

10 Penny Cole, "The Theme of Religious Pollution in Crusade Documents, 1095-1188," in *Crusaders and Muslims in Twelfth-Century Syria*, ed. Maya Shatzmiller (Leiden: Brill, 1993), 84-111 at 95.

liam of Tyre, who was otherwise horrified by the bloody capture of the holy city, repeated (relying on Albert of Aachen for his information) that the massacre was nonetheless "God's just judgement" and retribution for Muslim profanation of the holy sanctuary.[11]

The idea that crusaders were helping their brethren and the mother church—ideas of familial obligation—was quite commonly used by crusade preachers and propagandists of the early crusades, who also used biblical allusions to present the crusade as something of a rescue mission. The sort of gendered language that medieval writers used to talk about Jerusalem was supposed to inspire action by the city/church's children. This is why one dominant theme in crusade preaching is the theme of crusading as an act of love, as Jonathan Riley-Smith pointed out several decades ago. Love for the church and love for one's Christian family justified the use of violence as a sort of protective and retributive device against those who despoiled and endangered Christ's patrimony and the alleged rightful inheritance of all Christians.

Like the massacre of Jerusalem in 1099, the sack of Constantinople in 1204 by the armies of the Fourth Crusade is often cited as an example of the frenzied and uninhibited violence of crusading in general. Much of this view derives from the Greek sources, particularly those composed in Nicaea after the sack by refugees from Constantinople. Chief among these accounts is the *Historia* of Nicetas Choniates. Choniates had been a senior imperial official so not only was he highly educated and literate, but he was also deeply involved in the complex politics of the imperial environment. Choniates had moved to Nicaea in 1206/7, where the start of a Byzantine successor state was emerging, and wrote the portion of his *Historia* devoted to the fall and sack of Constantinople there.

Of Constantinople, Choniates famously wrote:

---

11 William of Tyre, *Chronicon*, ed. R. B. C. Huygens, H. E. Mayer and G. Rösch, Corpus Christianorum continuatio mediaevalis 63 (Turnhout: Brepols, 1986), 411–12.

O prolific city, once garbed in royal silk and purple and now filthy and squalid and heir to many evils, having need of true children! O city, formerly enthroned on high, striding far and wide, magnificent in comeliness and more becoming in stature; now your luxurious garments and elegant royal veils are rent and torn; your flashing eye has grown dark, and you are like an aged furnace woman all covered with soot and your formerly glistening and delightful countenance is now furrowed by loose wrinkles...this is the city, the crown and glory and joy of all the earth...how does the city that was filled with people sit as a widow and how has she, princess among provinces, become tributary?[12]

Much is striking about these words—the emotionally charged register, the rich and complex imagery, the biblical allusions. But there is also connection between the imagery of the city and the historical events of 1204. The Fourth Crusade (called in 1198) was initially meant to travel to the city of Alexandria in north Africa to disrupt the dominance of the Ayyubids there and thus open up the possibility of moving toward Jerusalem from the south. But a series of financial catastrophies in the tangled world of Mediterranean politics eventually diverted the crusading armies first to the port city of Zara (Zadar) on the Dalmatian coast (where some crusaders left the army to return home) and then to Constantinople.[13] The crusaders' arrival at Constantinople was tied up with their task of restoring the deposed emperor and his heir to the throne, and their presence in the city was initially supposed be something of a short stay until they might resume travel to Alexandria. Tensions arose, however, and the city was besieged and then finally invaded in April 1204. Much destruction ensued, including fire, three separate outbreaks of which consumed the besieged city in April and August of 1203 and then in April

---

12 *O City of Byzantium, Annals of Niketas Choniates*, trans. Harry J. Magoulias (Detroit: Wayne State University Press, 1984), 317.

13 Donald Queller and Thomas Madden, *The Fourth Crusade: The Conquest of Constantinople*, 2nd ed. (Philadephia: University of Pennsylvania Press, 1999).

1204 on the day the crusaders entered the city. The material and human consequences of these fires included the possible loss of some two hundred and fifty lives and the decimation of many homes—estimated to have been about one-sixth of the city. So when Choniates describes Constantinople as an "aged furnace woman all covered with soot," he certainly brings to mind the ash and soot that covered portions of the city as a result of the crusade.[14]

The imagery of the feminized city having been violated—"rent and torn"—also relates to the real violation of women reported during the sack of the city. Likening the city to a despoiled bride, Choniates also wrote of the crusaders as "implacable and crazed suitors" who had ignited "the coals of destruction" on both the physical space of the city and its inhabitants. Although oaths had been sworn that women and ecclesiastical buildings would be left alone during the sack of the city, these were ignored. Choniates tells us that there were efforts made by the men of the city to protect women and girls from rape, shielding them as they tried to flee, and that he himself prevented the rape of one young girl who was picked out of the group by a Latin. The theft of relics and the desecration of holy spaces by crusaders is perhaps the most well-known aspect of the sack of Constantinople. Choniates's text is therefore something of a lamentation for the city, and he consciously invokes the imagery of Jeremiah to emphasize both the scale of destruction and the blamelessness of this most Christian of cities. Like the representations of Jerusalem by crusade propagandists responding to the Muslim occupation of Jerusalem, Choniates's used established Christian tropes to communicate his outrage about Constantinople's fate, including imagery of the old woman, the queen, the mother, and the violated and despoiled woman. The feminization of the city thus connected Constantinople with

---

14 Jonathan Phillips, *The Fourth Crusade and the Sack of Constantinople* (London: Jonathan Cape, 2004). For the fires, see Thomas Madden, "The Fires of Fourth Crusade in Constantinople 1203–1204: A Damage Assessment," *Byzantinische Zeitschrift* 84–85 (1991–1992), 72–93.

a Christian past while simultaneously providing the language of critique for the crusaders' activities there.

That the sack of Constantinople has become a byword for brutality (as Michael Angold observed) is in large part due to the prominent place given to Choniates's narrative in histories of the Fourth Crusade.[15] Other contemporaneous texts certainly suggest that the violence was noteworthy: Pope Innocent III himself, although initially euphoric about the city's capture, later reprimanded crusade leaders for their brutality, while another contemporaneous text, the Latin eyewitness account known as the *Devastatio Constantinopolitana*, reported the "tremendous slaughter of the Greeks" and the fact that the looted treasures "filled three large towers with silver."[16] But the emotional rhetoric of Choniates's account has coloured many subsequent interpretations of the events of 1204 and at least part of the influence of this text, I would suggest, is its recourse to gendered tropes.

Broadly then, gendered language was a useful and meaningful tool with which medieval writers talked about and represented place and violence. Through images of cities as female, crusade propagandists and critics also described themes of duty, liberation, and the violation of Christian property. These sorts of themes also related to the notion of territorial entitlement on the grounds of righteous inheritance that underpinned the justification of crusading. At the same time, this sort of language was especially deployed (in the case of the Latin narratives) to resonate both with the knightly classes who were ideally the ones to undertake crusading activity and with the clerical and monastic audiences who preached and narrated the crusades from the outset. These were mostly male audiences. Violence could be justified both against "women" cities who were adulterers, and it

---

15 Michael Angold, *The Fourth Crusade* (London: Pearson, 2014).

16 Alfred J. Andrea, "The *Devastatio Constantinopolitana*, a Special Perspective on the Fourth Crusade: An Analysis, New Edition and Translation," *Historical Reflections/Réflexions historiques* 19, no. 1 (1993): 107–49 at 148.

could be justified to "rescue" assaulted women as an expression of social and familial obligation.

Creating Sacred Spaces

After the capture of Jerusalem in 1099, further waves of crusaders continued to arrive in the Holy Land. Some settled, others returned home. The so-called "crusader states" or "Outremer" which had been established during the First Crusade were vulnerable and over the course of the twelfth century shrank in territorial size. After the capture of Jerusalem itself by Saladin's armies in 1187 and with the new pontificate of Pope Innocent III from 1198, crusading increasingly came to be used against enemies other than Muslims and in locales other than the Holy Land, although Jerusalem remained both an important real and imagined destination for combatant and non-combatant crusaders. In the first quarter of the thirteenth century, crusades occurred in the Greek east, the south of France, the Baltic and northeastern Europe, in Egypt, and the Iberian Peninsula. All these locations were justified by crusade propagandists and participants as legitimate sites of crusading and the violence that accompanied it.

Part of the justification for crusading in locations other than the Holy Land was that these places were also spiritually significant. This allowed for the argument that such locales were, through the act of crusading, being purified, liberated, or restored to their proper status as Christian territory broadly understood. The reality was, of course, that most locations were not places where Christ had himself been physically present, nor were they necessarily easily associated with biblical history in general. The diversity of crusading locations from the twelfth century was therefore matched by efforts to justify the practice of holy war there. Such efforts included the physical transformation of places through crusading violence: in Jerusalem itself, the crusaders were said to have covered the Dome of the Rock with marble slabs and built an altar on it; in Egypt during the Fifth and Seventh Crusades, the mosque at the port city of Damietta was reconsecrated as a cathedral; a church was allegedly built over the top of a mass grave of murdered pagan farmers during the so-called Stedinger crusade of the 1230s. There are dozens of similar examples.

The Albigensian Crusade, which took place from 1209 to 1229 in the south of France—sometimes referred to as either Occitania or Languedoc, where Occitan was the principal language—is one example of how crusading violence was underpinned in part by the sacralization of space. This crusade was preached in the context of the perceived threat of heresy in the region, cumulatively stricter legislative and pastoral action by the Church against heresy during the later twelfth and early thirteenth centuries, the very localized and independent religious and political culture of the south of France, and the French Capetian royal house's rather tenuous authority over the region's aristocracy. The crusade itself was launched after preaching missions against the dualist so-called Cathar heretics who had become prominent in the region met with only limited success. The catalyst for military mobilization was the murder in 1208 of a papal legate, Pierre de Castelnau. Blame for this murder was attached to Raymond Count of Toulouse (suspected to be supportive of the heretics in his lands) and Pope Innocent III secured the agreement of the French king to use the instrument of crusade to eliminate heresy in the area. By 1209 the crusading army had assembled at Lyon and for the next several years, after an initial "shock and awe" strategy involving episodes of massacre, a war of attrition took place with some forty-five sieges against the region's towns until 1218. Gradually the main besieged towns submitted to the French crown and in 1229 the Treaty of Paris formally ended the crusade.[17]

The violence attached to this crusade is notorious, and is recorded in both contemporary sources and a large historiography. The crusade is quite distinctive for the range of

---

17 Lauren W. Marvin, *The Occitan War: A Military and Political History of the Albigensian Crusade, 1209-1218* (Cambridge: Cambridge University Press, 2008).

sources and perspectives that survive, including narrative sources in mostly chronicle form, songs from the singular "troubadour" culture of the Occitan world, and other documentary sources. This means that a fairly wide set of views about crusading violence have been recorded from "both sides" of the crusade. All agree that this was a brutal episode and that the violence enacted included both bodily violence, violence against sacred objects and sites, the displacement of people, and so on. Some episodes have become especially infamous: at Béziers in 1209, crusaders herded the citizens together and murdered nearly all of them. The city was looted, set on fire, and burned to the ground. Such events have been interpreted by some modern historians as excessive by the standards of medieval warfare, and by others as not dissimilar to other massacres between disparate groups in frontier areas at the same time. Others have described the event as the beginnings of genocide in the west, some have seen it as a deliberate and planned act of terror, and others have shown that, in military terms, the massacre at Béziers was spontaneous and mostly undirected. Conspiracy theorists have even used the crusade and its violence to support ideas about a homicidal Church, its secrets, fantasies, and nefarious plots.

Contemporary observers supportive of the crusade wrote narratives in which ideas about violence and legitimacy were very carefully delineated. Such narratives, including texts such as the *Historia Albigensis* of the eyewitness Peter of Les Vaux de Cernay, a monk who had accompanied his uncle on the Albigensian Crusade as well as the Fourth Crusade, represent the violence committed by the heretics as truly atrocious and excessive violence.[18] Peter reported that heretics desecrated the bodies of dead crusaders, murdered unarmed crusaders, smashed churches, and scattered the eucharistic host on the ground, mugged a priest and pissed on him, killed

---

18 *The History of the Albigensian Crusade: Peter of Les Vaux-de-Cernay's Historia Albigensis*, trans. W. A. and M. D. Sibly (Woodbridge: Boydell, 1998).

lords and assaulted a bishop, breaking his teeth. The violence committed by the crusaders, on the other hand, is depicted as the dispensation of justice, deployed with mercy, the performance of rightful retribution, and committed without pleasure by crusaders who had given the heretics every chance to repent. As with many other texts about crusading, miracles are included to show that God was, according to Peter, on the side of the crusaders: at Minerve in 1210 a slow flowing spring suddenly runs quickly, a wooden hut set alight refused to burn, crosses appeared on the walls of a church dedicated to Mary and then in the air, while a ghostly knight was seen to emerge from the city.

Peter's narrative does important cultural work in communicating ideas about proper and improper violence to the knightly and clerical audiences who may engage in crusading in the future or who wish to reflect on its past. He, like other medieval commentators, was keen to show the spiritual and canonical connections between brutality and justification for war, especially in the context of heresy, which from the late twelfth century had been defined as treason. In this way, the immediate and conceptual contexts in which the crusade occurred informed both its representation and its conduct. The territory itself as a site of miracles and trial spiritualized the landscape to link the actions of the crusading armies with the suffering of the Christian martyrs (Peter includes many references to the great persecutors of Christians, including Domitian and Diocletian). The crusaders' military strategy (apart from the extensive use of siege warfare) could also be described as a scorched earth policy which saw woods, vineyards, crops, and orchards destroyed, alongside castles and other buildings, and the displacement of populations. The transformation of the physical environment through destruction and depopulation ran alongside the construction of what we might call "orthodox space" in pro-crusade narratives. Imagery of the region as "the Lord's vineyard" was commonly employed by crusade preachers, and the heretics were said to be like foxes destroying the vines.

Troubadour culture in southern France is also an important context for what we might call public opinion on crusading. This was a courtly culture of song, and there are a large number of twelfth and thirteenth-century Occitanian songs concerned with telling the story of crusade and war, sometimes in celebration, sometimes with intense critique, sometimes with humour, and sometimes with a view to giving the conflicts "moral definition" of various partisan sorts. The *Song of the Cathar Wars* is one example.[19] This Occitan text offers a nice example of the polarization of opinion of the crusade as it was composed by two authors, one supportive of the crusade and another highly critical of it. The *Song of the Cathar Wars* narrates the sequence of war through its progress and impacts on both particular places and the generalized space of Occitania. The pro-crusade author (William of Tudela) writes the war through its sites of battle, including towns, meadows, plains, hillsides, and roadways, telling of martial successes and, at Béziers, the taking apart of the stone town walls and the unfortunate confusion that led to the burning of the church and the civilians within it. Massacre here is represented as partly tactical (a sign of strength and resolution), but also a product of the heat of battle (not entirely the fault of the crusaders).

The anonymous author of the second part of the *Song* evokes the fertility of the region to read the crusade as a fundamentally destructive effort—"they want to destroy us, they will harass us so that we cannot get this year's harvest in" (laisse 132). The idea that the crusaders are "destroying our inheritance" (laisse 133) is forefront; the Count of Toulouse is defeated "a landless man" (laisse 142). Impassioned speeches are reported to have been delivered by the Count's

---

19 Stephen G. Nichols, "Urgent Voices: The Vengeance of Images in Medieval Poetry," in *France and the Holy Land: Frankish Culture at the End of the Crusades*, ed. Daniel H. Weiss (Baltimore: Johns Hopkins University Press, 2004), 22–42; *The Song of the Cathar Wars. A History of the Albigensian Crusades*, ed. Janet Shirley (Aldershot: Ashgate, 1996).

vassals at the Fourth Lateran Council (1215) about the importance of place as inheritance (*eretatz*, in the Occitan), and its grievous loss as a result of the crusade. Violence done to places and peoples is narrated in this and other anti-crusade texts to describe a community bonded by shared *paratge* (a complex word signifying lineage, honour, community, and identity), which was unique and being eroded by this crusade. For other troubadours, this crusade was a distraction from crusades against other enemies in the Holy Land. This latter point also complicates the notion that the Albigensian crusade was a dichotomous conflict between "crusaders" and "heretics." There were many in the region who did not especially object to the instrument of crusade against enemies of the faith, but did not accept that those enemies were in Occitania. The problem was not necessarily the violence itself, but at whom it was directed.

Older historiographies read the violence of the Albigensian crusade as a product of the "real" motivation for it—that it was simply a land grab. There was clearly more to the crusade than this as the lengthy justifications underlining concern about heresy (whether perceived or actual) show. The Albigensian crusade was also singular in a number of ways: the span of crusade service was delineated (forty days), which meant a constantly changing set of military forces participated; the broader context of concern about the spread of heresy saw the secular arm being mobilized to oblige temporal rulers to rid their lands of heresy. In the context of crusade violence, it is also clear that place provided commentators with a useful lens through which to critique and support violence, using the language of tradition, including biblical and classical tropes, and the language of ownership, including Christian, familial, feudal, and regional claims to possession.

The testing ground for acceptable and unacceptable violence in war has often been identified as being border zones or frontiers, a phenomenon that has been extensively analyzed in the context of modern warfare and studies on why atrocities are committed. This is not the only space in which atrocities are committed, of course, and historians such as

Christopher Browning have shown that in their own back-yards people can succumb to pressures and commit actions they would never do of their own volition; that, in group settings, "ordinary men" will defer to authority, adapt to group activity, and create narratives about their actions that they can live with in order to explain atrocities committed.[20] Some military historians have identified individual disposition to violence, poor command discipline, novel situations, understandings of the need for group cohesion, and the emotional upheaval of transitioning from combat to aftermath as influencing behaviours. Others again identify the cultural contexts in which war is carried out as influencing the nature of its violence—the dehumanizing of enemies, hatred, vengeance, the breakdown of moral authorities that would normally limit violence, the feeling that one can "get away with it," and so on. In many modern cases, international laws or treaties of war do not prevent atrocities in military cultures where these conditions are found. The Geneva Conventions and the United Nations Convention against Torture, for instance, did not prevent the many atrocities against prisoners of war that took place at Abu Ghraib prison during the Iraq war of 2004. Such breaches of acceptable conduct can partly be explained by the location of war. Although atrocities take place in many locales, the violence in border zones or perceived frontiers—both physical and ideological—is often distinctive. This was true for some medieval conflicts, too, as may be illustrated by the case of crusading in the Baltic and northern Europe.

Missions to convert the pagan Wends (between the Elbe and Oder rivers) were underway at the same time as the First Crusade was preached to Jerusalem, and over the course of the twelfth and thirteenth centuries, the practice and language of holy war infiltrated military, conversion, and colonization activity across the Baltic. As early as 1108, the so-called "Magdeburg Charter," a document with a murky

---

20 Christopher Browning, *Ordinary Men: Reserve Police Battalion 101 and the Final Solution in Poland*, rev. ed. (New York: HarperCollins, 2017).

history (probably the work of a cleric, addressed to all Christians, but possibly with no official capacity) called for a holy war to convert pagans and to defend local Christians in the Baltic region and beyond. This is a significant document in many ways but for the purposes of this chapter it is especially noteworthy for its framing of northern Europe as "our Jerusalem." A crusade against the Wends took place at the same time as the Second Crusade (1147) and is often considered one of the "arms" of this crusade which also included the conquest of Lisbon and a failed journey to the Levant. A series of missions to conquer and Christianize Livonia (on the eastern coast of the Baltic Sea), was launched at the end of the twelfth century, while throughout the thirteenth century, numerous missions occurred in Livonia, Estonia, Finland, and Prussia.

The links between these sorts of missions and crusading were sometimes unclear, as the aspect of pilgrimage that was so important to crusades to the Holy Land, for instance, was absent. Yet contemporary chroniclers were determined to describe these journeys as such, with writers such as Henry of Livonia (writing ca. 1225–1226) and Arnold of Lübeck (writing ca. 1209–1214) writing that participants were marked with the sign of the cross, were protecting Christendom generally (and missionaries and new converts in particular) from the ravages of the "pagans," and were undertaking a sacred journey as pilgrims for the same spiritual benefits as those who travelled to the Holy Land.[21] Singular in these missions was the aspect of forced conversion, which was not part of the preaching of the early crusades to the Holy Land and indeed contravened medieval canon law, but which had gained some traction in the Wendish Crusade as one motivating principle. It was not until the Livonian Crusade that this motivation brought together crusade and mission overtly; even so, the language of protecting Christians and spreading the Christian faith was used in papal letters about these mis-

---

21 *The Chronicle of Arnold of Lubeck*, trans. Graham Loud (London: Routledge, 2019); *The Chronicle of Henry of Livonia*, trans. James Brundage (New York: Columbia University Press, 2003).

sions, although on the ground, the reality seems to have also included forced conversions.

Christian narratives about the Livonian Crusade also worked hard to fashion the region as a space that was essentially Christian despite its lack of a long Christian history, and a space that was able to be overlaid with Christianity by the presence and actions of the conversion missions and the instrument of crusade. Marek Tamm has showed that this was achieved in Livonia by representing the region as a new "promised land" and by closely associating it with the Virgin Mary.[22] Arnold of Lübeck thought that a crusade to protect the Christians in the area could be equated with the liberation of Jerusalem, as the region for him was like a new Jerusalem, fertile and rich, and something of an earthly paradise. As Marek Tamm pointed out, although the equation of Livonia with the Holy Land may seem a stretch for the modern reader, the representation of this locale where preachers had been and which was "fertile in fields, plentiful in pastures, irrigated by rivers...rich in fish and forested by trees" created the idea that this was a promised land (446). Both Arnold of Lübeck and Henry of Livonia were especially keen to link the region with the presence and patronage of Mary, describing miracles where she healed a lame knight who wished to participate in the crusade, noting her special patronage of newly founded episcopal sees, dedications of holy buildings to her, and representing Livonia as her dowry, rather like the Holy Land was often described by crusade propagandists as Christ's patrimony.

Like in Languedoc, historians often characterize crusade activity in Livonia as being especially violent. Similarly, the violence is represented in the contemporary sources as occurring "on both sides," but with different overlaying interpretations. As the heretics in Peter of Les Vaux de Cernay's *Historia Albigensis* are described as particularly brutal,

22 Marek Tamm, "How to Justify a Crusade? The Conquest of Livonia and New Crusade Rhetoric in the Early Thirteenth Century," *Journal of Medieval History* 39, no. 4 (2013): 431–55.

so the Baltic "pagans" (an amorphous category mostly, but sometimes delineated by ethnic categorization, such as "the Letts") are supposed to have delighted in cruelty, practising "unbelievable torments" on Christians, roasting people alive, cutting the shape of crosses into their flesh, stabbing splinters underneath their fingernails. Tales of atrocity like these are intended to show the barbarous otherness of these groups just as much as they are intended to show the conditions in which martyrdom might be achieved for the crusader and missionary victims of violence. These tales themselves create a sacred landscape populated by the memory of Christians who died there in defence of Christendom—perhaps a destination for future pilgrimage.

The violence inflicted on the pagans, on the other hand, is unsurprisingly legitimate, just, and divinely and institutionally supported. When the severed head of Ako, a Livonian leader, was sent to the bishop as a sign of victory, there was much rejoicing. At one point, the Virgin Mary herself is an agent of violence, according to Henry of Livonia's chronicle, which describes how she "always guards Livonia" by striking with sudden death, humiliating, or driving out those who despoil "her special land" (chapter 25 of Henry of Livonia's chronicle). Henry also uses the well-rehearsed image of the Maccabees to equate the soldiers in Livonia not only with these biblical exemplars, but also with previous crusaders who had been, from the preaching of the First Crusade, linked with these biblical warriors.

The conditions in which the crusade ventures of the twelfth and thirteenth centuries occurred in the Baltic have been identified by historians as one reason for the particularly savage nature of the violence committed there. Crusaders signed up for a period of service of one year as a minimum for the so-called Livonian Crusade at the end of the twelfth century (this term of service predated the forty-day term that was a feature of the Albigensian crusade from 1209 to 1229). They were not accompanied by a papal legate, as had been the case in previous crusades, where someone representing papal interests, preaching the crusade, and overseeing the actions of the crusaders would be physically present with the crusaders for varying lengths of time. Whether or not this would have had a moderating influence on the actions of crusading armies is a little speculative given the patchy record of legates in this regard, but it is not a stretch to imagine that, as James Brundage noted some time ago, the main task of these crusading legates was "to see that the actions of the crusaders were kept in line with the objectives of the papacy in sanctioning the crusade."[23] The initiative for the crusade came principally from Bishop Albert of Riga, rather than from the pope at the outset (although of course it was indeed papally sanctioned). Thus, there were some unusual factors present in this "holy war"—limited service, local organization, and no accompanying papal legate at the start. By the time Henry of Livonia had composed his chronicle a legate did appear in Livonia, so the latter feature did certainly change.

Did this mean that those who participated in the mission may have been "unregulated" until the arrival of the legate (William of Modena)? The main source for information is Henry's *Chronicle* which, as with all the other narrative representations of crusade violence, is a mediated account meant to stimulate particular responses for particular audiences. So it must be read with a view to recognizing the tropes he felt resonated with his readers, for instance. Henry represents the crusade as a defensive war against those "pagans" who both threatened the church generally and other Christians who had recently been converted in the region. The crusade was also directed at apostates, local people who had converted to Christianity but reverted to "paganism" once they could. For Henry of Livonia, this was legitimate reason for forced re-conversion as apostasy was considered to be especially heinous. His emphasis on martyrdom, too, may hint at the violent context in which these crusade missions operated.

---

23 James Brundage, "The Thirteenth-Century Livonian Crusade: Henricus de Lettis and the First Legatine Mission of Bishop. William of Modena," *Jahrbücher für Geschichte OstEuropas* 20, no. 1 (1972): 1–9 at 5.

Again, using well-rehearsed tropes from tales of ancient martyrs, Henry emphasized the barbarity of the enemy as well as showing the eternal rewards for the mostly German and local converts who were deemed martyrs for their efforts. All this went to representing the crusade mission broadly as a just and holy war while revealing something of its practice and composition.

One particular feature of warfare in the Baltic was the presence of the military orders. These orders arose in the aftermath of the First Crusade as a defensive force to protect pilgrims to holy places in the Holy Land. They were distinctive in following monastic vows as well as being knights—a "new knighthood" as the Cistercian abbot Bernard of Clairvaux wrote in a mid-twelfth century treatise in praise of the Knights Templar—and by the end of the twelfth century, the Templars and other orders, including the Hospitallers, flourished in the Holy Land (although not without political and military stresses especially around the time of the loss of Jerusalem in 1187 and the Third Crusade). The Teutonic knights, founded in the Holy Land in the aftermath of the Third Crusade in the 1190s and especially active from the time of the Fifth Crusade, had been granted in 1226 the right to control any lands it conquered from the Prussians. This prompted what would become the foundation of the Teutonic knights' Prussian state. It is worth mentioning this novelty in the context of the sacralization of the landscape, as the Teutonic knights were unique in this regard. They were able to grant crusade indulgences without papal authorization (from 1245), and they were able to develop the institution of crusade in support of their state as what Christopher Tyerman described as an instrument of foreign policy. The Teutonic knights carved out a physical and spiritual space for themselves in the crusading world, eventually hosting crusaders on a quasi-seasonal basis in their mission to conquer territory in Lithuania and Poland well into the fifteenth century.

Conclusion

In this chapter, I have looked at four well-known examples of crusading violence—the capture of Jerusalem in 1099, the sack of Constantinople in 1204, the Albigensian crusade from 1209, and crusades against the pagans in the twelfth and thirteenth centuries—to show that ideas of space were an important part of the cultural vocabulary of crusading violence. It is clear that to start unravelling how crusading violence was thought to be justified in different situations, it is important to explore how it was represented in the sources which narrated or critiqued it. I have suggested here that close reading of those sources reveals the various rhetorical and literary means by which the meaning and contexts of violence are communicated. Such things as gendered language or biblical imagery are not just flourishes in these texts. They are the windows into the medieval worlds in which violence garnered meaning and was performed, consciously and thoughtfully. Reading crusading as a spatial practice illuminates how the language of pollution/purification could be deployed to rationalize possession and violence, too.

But, of course, violence was never only rhetorical and violence inflicted on people was not simply an aesthetic construct. In the next chapter, I look more closely at violence committed against physical bodies, and how legitimate targets of crusader violence were identified.

Chapter 2

Bodies and Violence

Recently Hannah Skoda has emphasized the idea that medieval violence was a form of communication which, like other forms of communication, possessed "shared norms and conventions: or grammars" (*Medieval Violence*, 18). The idea that violence communicates something that is founded on shared codes of meaning is a useful point from which to proceed when exploring *who* was understood to be a legitimate target of crusading violence during the central Middle Ages. In so doing, we find that crusade justifications of violence toward specific groups and individuals were also built on shared ideas and assumptions about the nature and meaning of the physical body. These ideas and assumptions created what we might describe as the "behavioural scripts" of violence; that is, the practice, conduct, and communication of social and cultural norms through the exercise of violence.

An extensive literature on the medieval body over the last decades has analyzed the body's fluidity, connection to spiritual states, performativity, medicalization—its legibility, as Skoda and others have explained. The contexts that shaped such bodily states or categories (theology, law, centres of learning, custom and tradition, the family, storytelling, and so on) also shaped cultures of crusading, itself a vehicle for bringing together and playing out a whole range of ideas about the body in its formulation and practice. Clearly, there was never a singular "medieval attitude toward the body." But in the western intellectual, Christian, and Latinate cultures of the twelfth and thirteenth centuries, there were certainly shared understandings of the body and its meanings. These informed the thought-worlds of crusading. Indeed, to think about meanings and manifestations of crusading violence is to dive deep into the complexity of attitude toward different medieval bodies. Focussing on the idea of the body helps us to understand how crusade violence was fundamentally corporeal in every aspect.

The body was central to the mission of the crusade in three main ways. The body of the "other" was constructed as a legitimate target of violence; the body of the crusader was constructed as the appropriate instrument through which crusading was practised and reified; and the body of Christ was a central motif to the justification and practice of crusading violence. We might also think about the importance of intention when it came to bodily violence in crusading warfare. What was violence against particular bodies meant to achieve? Why violence, indeed, and not something else? What, precisely, was to be communicated by doing violence to a body? How did certain bodies function as legitimate sites of violence?

It might be imagined that such regulations as military ordinances would reveal how bodily violence was ordered, and it is true that such ordinances existed for individual crusades from the twelfth century. Although these were not universal in reach or application, ideas of restraint were communicated to armies and their leaders by campaign-specific regulations. In crusading contexts, such regulations covered a range of issues, including the settlement of disputes, sexual conduct, sumptuary rules, crimes such as theft, as well as rules around military cohesion. Frederick Barbarossa's ordinances on the Third Crusade, for example, dealt with behaviour such as cheating and fraud, as did the rules agreed to by Henry II and Richard I of England for the same crusade which also addressed gambling, debt, swearing, and other potential infringements. Some historians have linked such attempts to regulate military discipline with a medieval culture of chivalry where the exercise of violence could be legitimate in formal contexts, while more recently, Christopher Tyerman has linked such regulations with the creation of a "political space" in military settings, where relationships of negotiation and influence were forged and tested.[1] But such ordinances were mostly directed at internal discipline and were only infrequently concerned with the question of violence toward non-combatants or others. This meant that ideas about the regulation of bodily violence cannot be sought in these sorts of disciplinary texts alone.

Thus, this chapter looks at the corporeality of crusade violence more broadly. I begin by looking at well-known victims of crusade violence and prevalent ideas about the crusader's own body to suggest that violence was not something that was only imagined as a punitive or vengeful instrument against "out groups." Crusade violence was imagined through all bodies, including the crusader's own body. This argument is meant to indicate, too, that explaining crusade violence simply as a product of hostility toward non-Christian groups is not quite enough to explain why bodily violence was so central to the crusade imaginary. A Christian cultural emphasis in the twelfth and thirteenth centuries on the suffering body, longer histories of religious practice involving bodily regulation and correction (including forms of monastic life), as well as evolving notions of bodily and spiritual difference all informed both crusading attitudes toward the body and the centrality of the body in the communication of crusading purposes and ideas. Violence done to and by the physical body was integral to all aspects of crusading, not just in military or combat settings. It was the means by which the penitential and punitive aspects of crusading could be brought together.

Victims of Violence

Although the First Crusade was principally directed at Muslims in the Holy Land to achieve the "liberation" of Jerusalem,

---

1 Christopher Tyerman, "Commoners on Crusade: the Creation of Political Space?," *English Historical Review* 136, no. 579 (2021): 245–75.

the first victims of crusading violence were neither Muslim nor in the Levant. It was the Jewish communities in the Rhine valley that experienced the first violence of the crusading enterprise when, beginning in early May 1096, groups of crusaders massacred Jewish communities in Speyer, Worms, Mainz, Metz, Cologne, Trier, Regensburg, and Prague. These attacks also involved the destruction and looting of property including burning synagogues and destroying sacred texts and objects, while some Jews were forced to choose to convert to Christianity or to die. The mass suicides in some of these communities by those who refused this choice are well-known. As far as we know, attacking Jews was not part of the preaching of the First Crusade, and some Christian leaders condemned and prohibited this violence; the bishop attempted to protect the Jewish community in Speyer, for example. Yet still the attacks occurred and, like the episodes of violence I outlined in the previous chapter (the sack of Constantinople, the massacre at Béziers, and the capture of Jerusalem), the violence committed against the Rhineland Jews in 1096 occupies a central place in the historiography and memory of crusading violence. In Jewish history and memory, the massacres left an indelible mark: three medieval Jewish prose accounts document the massacres (the so-called Mainz Anonymous account, the account of Solomon b. Samson, and the account of Eliezer b. Nathan), and other literary forms reflect on it including exegetical commentary and liturgical poetry. Indeed, the literary space that was produced as a result of these events has been described as a "turning point in the literary history of European Judaism."[2] The Christian sources for the massacres are sparser, with only two contemporary crusade chronicles—Albert of Aachen's *Historia Hierosolymitana* (mostly composed in the early years of the twelfth century) and the chronicle tradition associated with

---

2 Uri Zvi Shachar, "Hebrew Crusade Literature in Its Latin and Arabic Contexts," in *The Cambridge Companion to the Literature of the Crusades*, ed. Anthony Bale (Cambridge: Cambridge University Press, 2018), 102–18 at 103.

Frutolf of Michelsberg (between 1108 and 1130)—describing the events in any detail.[3]

Academic interpretations of the Rhineland massacres are diverse. Some emphasize that the acts were a distortion of the crusade so must be distinguished from it; others link it to general discourses of persecution that both underpinned the crusade and reached beyond it to all marginalized groups. Historians have explored ideas that this violence was meant to cleanse or purify, that it was part of the apocalyptic discourse embedded in the First Crusade, that it was the inevitable consequence of a long history of violence against Jews given a new outlet with the preaching of the crusade. Jonathan Riley-Smith argued that at the root of the violence was the implied justification that it was somehow righteous, and meant to avenge Christ's crucifixion. Such analyses of motive have shown how long histories of religious difference, precedents for violence, opportunity, and perceived justification were brought together in the events of 1096. Careful studies of the Jewish narratives have recently responded to earlier and teleological views that the massacres were a part of a long history of anti-Jewish persecution that would lead to the Holocaust, by considering them as literary texts designed to enshrine and encode memory with religious, didactic purposes.

The violence of 1096 certainly marked something of an escalation of various forms of bodily and rhetorical violence against Jews across the medieval west, especially in France and England. Although the twelfth century saw an increase of the circulation and knowledge of the Talmud in western Europe, it also saw the development of the myths of host desecration and ritual murder and eventually the blood libel accusations of the thirteenth century. Attacks on Jews occurred as these and other stories spread. As has been well documented, there existed a variety of often inconsistent

---

3 It is certainly worth mentioning that Guibert of Nogent also described a pogrom that occurred in Normandy which he connects to the crusade. See Guibert of Nogent, *De vita sua sive monodiae*, ed. E.-R. Labande (Paris: Belle Lettres, 1981), 246–48.

responses by ecclesiastical authorities to violence against Jews—sometimes Jews were protected and sometimes they were condemned. Lay reactions were similarly consistent as David Nirenberg has recently shown in his major work on anti-Judaism, where he usefully notes that "the Middle Ages created for the Jews a political and legal status analogous to their hermeneutic one" (*Anti-Judaism*, 193). In other words, Jews were both marginalized and used for the benefit of sovereign power. This was most apparent in France, where Jews undertook economic activities prohibited for Christians, such as money lending, which benefited the monarchy's finances through taxation. The association between Jews, the monarchy, and money had the effect of making violence committed against Jews an attack on power itself, not just an attack on a religious group broadly identified as non-normative.

Historical explanations for the massacres have also emphasized the theological idea of "witness." This is the Augustinian theory that Jews were needed to remind Christians of the consequences of rejecting Christ: for Jews this consequence was their dispersal around the world. At the same time, the presence of Jews in Christian societies was the embodiment of the idea that their conversion would herald the end times, as foretold in biblical prophecy. These ideas meant that Jews were understood to be witnesses to past events and to serve social and eschatological purposes: they served their lords through the payment of taxes, and they were thought to serve Christendom by acting as witnesses to and agents of Christian history. The idea that Jews were essential to Christendom retained its force throughout the crusading period: in 1146, the Cistercian abbot and vociferous supporter of the crusade, Bernard of Clairvaux, sent a letter to the clergy and people of east France and Bavaria and an almost identical letter to the people of England in support of the Second Crusade in which he differentiated between Jews and Muslims, describing the latter as "enemies of the cross" and "pagan filth." Bernard's comments on Jews were also condemnatory, arguing that Jews rejected Christ so deserved to be scattered. But he also wrote that Jews should not be murdered by crusaders as they are needed to fulfil the Scriptural prophecy that they will eventually be converted (Romans 11:26). This prohibition against killing Jews was not, therefore, a reflection of what we might think of as an ethical position against violence, but rather was based on the same religious arguments that marginalized Jews in Christian thought. When the twelfth-century Jewish scholar Ephraim of Bonn reported that Bernard said: "Whosoever touches a Jew to take his like is like one who harms Jesus himself..., for in the book of Psalms it is written of them, 'Slay them not, lest my people forget,'" he reminded his medieval audience that Bernard did not think that violence was wrong in principle, but that Jews were needed to fulfil their function of witness in the Augustinian scheme.[4]

Papal responses to anti-Jewish violence stirred by the preaching of the crusade should also be understood to have emerged from a similar framing. The papal bull *Sicut Iudeis* issued between 1119 and 1124 by Pope Calixtus II (although originally emanating from Pope Gregory I in the sixth century and reissued many times during the Middle Ages), declared that violence against Jews to force them into baptism was forbidden as was other violence, robbery, or disturbance of Jewish religious celebrations. Jews were offered papal protection— but only Jews who were not thought "to plot against the Christian faith." This piece of legislation is not an overarching or unchanging "medieval papal policy" toward Jews, as Rebecca Rist has shown. It was a reaction to continued outbreaks of violence against Jews when crusades were preached, sometimes at the request of local Jewish communities themselves. It ran alongside variegated political and social attitudes which ranged from the protections offered by monarchs like Louis VII

---

4 *Sancti Bernardi Opera*, ed. J. Leclercq, H. Rochais, and C. H. Talbot, 8 vols. (Rome: Editiones Cistercienses, 1957–1977), 8:311–17; *Sefer Zekhirah* or *The Book of Remembrance of Rabbi Ephraim of Bonn* in *The Jews and the Crusaders: The Hebrew Chronicles of the First and Second Crusades*, trans. and ed. Shlomo Eidelberg (Madison: University of Wisconsin Press, 1977; repr., 1996), 122.

of France (1137–1180), who granted Jews the right to build new synagogues, to the expulsions ordered by Philip Augustus of France (1179–1223), which occurred almost at the exact time that Pope Alexander III prohibited throwing objects at Jews during religious processions in 1179.[5]

Cultural attitudes toward Jews replicated the ambiguous but generally negative framing of legislative and theological representations but drew new force from twelfth-century scholars like Peter the Venerable who thought that "Jews who live in our midst, blaspheme, abuse and trample on Christ" and wondered why Christians should travel to "far and distant lands" in pursuit of the enemies of Christ when "far worse than any Muslims, namely the Jews" were so much closer to home.[6] Among these ideas was the idea that Jewish bodies were distinctive. The Jewish body was represented as weakened by the ritual of circumcision which was thought to be both emasculating and evidence that Jews stubbornly adhered to a ritual that was superfluous after the baptism of Christ. Jewish bodies were associated with leprosy and they were suspected of wanting to bathe in the blood of innocents to cure it; they were thought to have a unique physiognomy; they were said to be prone to melancholy and illness as they refused the healing power of baptism. Jews were thought to be highly sexualized and even licentious. These ideas were not uniformly delineated during the crusading period, but they were part of a package of attitudes across western Europe that circulated in text, sermon, and visual culture, in tropes such as the *synagoga/ecclesia* dichotomy, where the idea was communicated in sculptural form on the exterior of some churches that adherents to the Old Testament were blind (*synagoga*) while those who followed the Gospel (*ecclesia*) were seeing.

---

5 Rebecca Rist, *Popes and Jews, 1095–1291* (Oxford: Oxford University Press, 2015).

6 Peter the Venerable, *Against the Inveterate Obduracy of the Jews*, trans. I. Resnick (Washington, DC: Catholic University of America Press).

The massacres of 1096 were thus both part of a longer story of assumptions about Jews and part of a differentiated vocabulary of violence that proliferated throughout the high Middle Ages. The crusaders and pilgrims who participated in the massacres had a range of sometimes contested discourses from which to draw and although the surviving versions of Pope Urban II's sermon do not report him preaching that Jews alongside Muslims were the legitimate targets of crusade violence, it has long been recognized that the instrument of holy war was easy to unroll against Jews, too. Jewish texts report that "those signed with the cross" and "pilgrims" took part in the violence as they believed that they should exact vengeance on those "who killed and crucified Him." Some have called the perpetrators "popular crusaders," others have described them as a greedy mob, and older historiographies identified them vaguely with "the peasants' crusade"—men somehow separate from the crusade army proper. Those who grouped around Count Emicho of Flonheim at Speyer were joined at Mainz by crusaders from other part of Germany, France, England, and the Low Countries, while it seems that at Regensburg it was the army gathered around Peter the Hermit that forced mass conversions to Christianity. But these were all crusaders who shared a common understanding that bodies were legitimate targets of violence. The violence against the Rhineland Jews was not an aberration, nor was it somehow separate from the violence legitimized by the language of vengeance attributed to Urban. The umbrella of the crusade and all the existing prejudices meant that there existed already a plethora of social and cultural support for physical marginalization, including murder, of this group.

Violence committed against various Muslim groups was also represented by crusade preachers and polemicists as being necessary for the good of Christendom on the grounds that Muslims persecuted Christians and unjustly occupied holy places (particularly but not exclusively Jerusalem). Although Muslim possession of these holy places had existed for some four hundred years prior to the preaching of the

First Crusade, the devotional environment of eleventh-century Christianity sparked resistance toward the idea that this should continue. Who was exactly meant by "Saracens" was not always clear and all sorts of groups came to be lumped together under this broad category in the polemical and pro-crusade texts of the high Middle Ages. The term "Saracen," one of a number of ethnic significations deriving from late antique geographers who thought that Muslims were Arabs who descended from Ishmael, the illegitimate son of Hagar (Sarah's handmaid), and Abraham, came to be pejoratively applied to Muslims during the time of the crusades, and the term likewise was something of a catch-all for a variety of groups.[7] One Spanish crusading song known as "Ay Iherusalem" is a good example, identifying the enemy generally as "Moors," but then including other groups in this general category (Tartars, Ethiopians, Africans, and Egyptians—called Babylonians here). Rachel Golden has shown that other crusade songs were similarly various in their categorization of the "enemy" of crusaders, some grouping Saracens and Jews as the opposite of Christian, and some clearly aware of different groups such as Berbers, Moroccans, and others, but still thinking of them (and singing them) collectively as Saracens or Arabs or Moors.[8]

Underpinning hostility to these groups was also hostility to non-Christians, loosely categorized in many cases. In the great crusading bull of 1187 issued in response to the battle of Hattin, *Audita tremendi*, Pope Gregory VIII called for a crusade to recapture Jerusalem, recently lost to the armies of Salah-ad-Din, in which he equated Muslims with pagans who were bent on profaning the holy to erase the name of

---

7 John Tolan, *Saracens: Islam in the Medieval European Imagination* (New York: Columbia University Press, 2002), xix. Tolan notes that the construction of a polemical image of Saracens started before the rise of Islam and that Islamic tradition also includes the idea that Arabs were descended from Ishmael.

8 Rachel Golden, *Mapping Medieval Identities in Occitanian Crusade Song* (Oxford: Oxford University Press, 2020); Tolan, *Saracens*.

God. This sort of characterization was common in crusading polemic as a way of "framing the holy war in terms of spiritual opposition," as Katherine Smith stated, by constructing the Saracen other as idolatrous.[9] At the same time, Muslims were sometimes represented as heretics. One preacher of the Fifth Crusade, Oliver of Paderborn, thought that because Muslims deny Christ's passion and death and the union of his human and divine natures, they "ought to be called heretics rather than Saracens."[10] The clerical notion that Islam was a "false religion" did not change dramatically throughout the period of twelfth and thirteenth-century crusades, even when there was much more knowledge about Islam and many more direct encounters with Muslims. In fact, the old polemics just became more embedded and sometimes more vitriolic during this time.

The very anthropological position of Muslims was called into question in some twelfth-century clerical texts, partially as a result of these homogenizing taxonomies attached to Islam and Muslims in general. The Anglo-Norman cleric, Orderic Vitalis, called Muslims "creatures of another race"[11] (*allophili*), while others equated them with animals and insects. A letter from Terricus, a senior Templar, after the Battle of Hattin in 1187 reported that the "horde of pagans" is so great that they are "like a swarm of ants covering this whole face of the earth"; others thought that collectively, these groups were "inhuman," "dogs." The characterization of Muslims as reproducing uncontrollably also underpinned justifications of violence done to them, as Christians thought that Muslims were polyamorous and thus preoccupied with the body. The thirteenth-century Dominican preacher Humbert of Romans

---

9 Katherine Allen Smith, *The Bible and Crusade Narrative in the Twelfth Century* (Woodbridge: Boydell and Brewer, 2020), 134.

10 Oliver of Paderborn, "The Capture of Damietta," in Bird, Peters, and Powell, eds., *Crusade and Christendom*, 179.

11 Orderic Vitalis, *Historia Ecclesiastica*, ed. and trans. M. Chibnall, 6 vols. (Oxford: Oxford University Press, 1969–1980), bk. 9, ch. 2 (vol. 5, p. 16).

said that it was preferable to commit violence against Muslims and that missions against them ought to be abandoned because there is no hope of converting them: "as long as they remain in the world, they will multiply without measure unless they are destroyed by some Christian or barbarian power." Humbert repeated the well-known phrase from Matthew 26:52, "He who lives by the sword will perish by the sword," to say that Muhammed spread Islam by the sword so Muslims should die by it.[12]

Humbert of Romans was also building on a tradition of crusade propaganda that represented Muslims as themselves practising a particularly cruel variety of anti-Christian violence. From the earliest narrative accounts of Pope Urban II's 1095 sermon at Clermont, crusade texts regularly included reports of what was described as "unheard of cruelty" done to Christians and holy places, tortures, savagery, and slaughter. The rich historiography of such narratives (chronicles, but also letters and sermons) reminds us that exaggerated reporting served both the stylistic purpose of engaging an audience as well as serving as counter-propaganda. That is, narrating the violence that Muslims did to Christian bodies and Christian places was intended to justify the scale of violence committed against them, explaining the vengeful premise underpinning the preaching of the early crusades. Similarly violent imagery can be found in crusade songs such as "Ay Iherusalem," in which the lyrics graphically narrate that "The Christians see their sons roasted, / they see their wives' breasts sliced off; / they go along the streets / with their hands and feet cut off / in Jerusalem. / They made blankets out of the vestments; / they made a stable out of the Holy Sepulchre; / with the holy crosses /

---

12 Orderic Vitalis, *Historia Ecclesiastica*, bk. 9, ch. 4 (vol. 5); Letter from Terricus to Henry II of England, in Malcolm Barber and Keith Bate, trans. and ed., *Letters from the East: Crusaders, Pilgrims and Settlers in the 12th and 13th Centuries* (Aldershot: Ashgate, 2010), 83–84; Humbert of Romans in Bird, Peters, and Powell, eds., *Crusade and Christendom*, 457–58.

they made stakes / in Jerusalem."[13] This particular song was composed as something of a lament for the holy city after its capture by the Khwarezmians in 1244, but echoes clearly the sort of language employed by earlier crusade writers to stimulate anger and outrage and thereby promote the action of crusade. Other reports of the 1244 capture of Jerusalem also emphasize the cruelty of the Khwarezmians, one report telling of "the intolerable atrocity" of nuns and aged and infirm men having their throats cut in the church of the holy sepulchre "thus perpetrating in his holy sanctuary such a crime as the eyes of men had never seen since the commencement of the world."[14]

The notion that hostile people were being punished is one explanation for violence against them. When Damietta was captured during the Fifth Crusade after a long siege, Oliver of Paderborn wrote that the city was "subjected to manifold punishments [and] the Lord struck them down without sword of fire, scorning henceforth to endure the uncleanness committed in you."[15] The disease and famine within the city that was caused by the siege were cast by Oliver as instruments of divine anger and although he reported the "wretched sight" that confronted the crusaders when they finally entered the city, Oliver was keen to represent these civilian deaths as part of God's wrath and legitimate punishment. He quotes Isaiah 14:5 and Psalm 74: 11: "The Lord hath broken the staff of the wicked. He hath broken the horn of the proud; he who above the sons of men is terrible" (191). Likewise, crusade propaganda emphasized the idea that it was an affront to Christians and to God that holy places be occupied by Muslims. The Holy Land itself was said to have been "spattered with Christ's blood...and now experiences the lash at enemy hands more harshly...worn down by hammer blows of perse-

---

13 Golden, *Mapping Medieval Identities*, 39.

14 Matthew Paris, "The Sack of Jerusalem, 1244," in Bird, Peters, and Powell, eds., *Crusade and Christendom*, 301.

15 Oliver of Paderborn, "The Capture of Damietta," in Bird, Peters, and Powell, eds., *Crusade and Christendom*, 187.

cution which is hers and ours..." according to Pope Innocent
IV in a letter to Henry III of England in 1245. "Is the wickedness of that people to go unpunished?," Innocent wondered,
"are they to be allowed freely to run amok with the sword?'[16]
Righteous zeal and punishment were, for Innocent IV and
dozens of other crusade propagandists, legitimate motivations for holy war generally and violence against Muslim bodies in particular.

Violence and Corporeality: Interpretations

The polemic framing of Jews and Muslims as "other" is very
easy to rehearse, as I have done above. Indeed, it remains a
dominant interpretive framework for explaining the violence
of crusading against certain groups. This partly derives from
an influential historiographical moment in the late twentieth
century, R. I. Moore's idea of "the persecuting society," a
landmark study (since revised and updated) of the rhetorical
and material ways in which, from the period of the Gregorian
reforms, Latin Christian society grew more discriminatory,
more violent, more punitive in its treatment of those deemed
to be outside the community of the faithful.[17] As the examples
I have outlined above would indicate, it is not difficult to see
the construction of the other in medieval Christian (mostly
clerical) imaginings of its own terrestrial and eternal parameters—"Christendom"—during the high Middle Ages. For
some decades now, Moore's framework has been critiqued
for universalizing ideas and attitudes across what were actually quite distinctive and disparate regional cultures, and for
paying scant attention to the lived realities of coexistence
and interaction between disparate religious groups, including
in the Holy Land. Recent work accepts the marginalization of

16 Peter Jackson, trans., *The Seventh Crusade, 1244-1254: Sources
and Documents* (Aldershot: Ashgate, 2009), 25.

17 R. I. Moore, *The Formation of a Persecuting Society: Authority and
Deviance in Western Europe, 950-1250*, 2nd ed. (1987; Oxford: Oxford
University Press, 2007).

certain groups within Latin Christian cultures, but has looked to a range of sources and experiences to uncover the many other forms of contact and encounter that existed alongside times of hostility and violence. One example is Christopher MacEvitt's work on the "rough tolerance" that existed among Latin and Eastern Christian groups in the crusader states, which provides a useful framework with which to consider the variety and historical specificities of interactions and encounters during periods of instability.[18]

Geraldine Heng has recently used the category of race to explain strategies and reasons for medieval marginalization and violence more generally. Heng argued that racialized thinking was not a product of modernity and that such thinking underpinned medieval interactions and shaped identities, including through crusading. For Heng, violence is thus a "logical consequence...of the dynamics of race identity in a global holy war where religion is defined through categories of blood."[19] So for instance, when some of the First Crusade chronicles (the *Gesta Francorum*, Fulcher of Chartres's *Historia Hierosolymitana*) narrate violence done to Muslims and others during the capture of Jerusalem in 1099, their narratives reduce "human bodies to mere thinghood," dehumanizing Muslims as objects not people. Although Heng's claim that "crusaders [were] a virtual race in global war" (124) perhaps universalizes "crusaders" too emphatically (what do we do with Muslim mercenaries who fought with Christians in Spain and north Africa, for instance?, were heretics in the south of France also represented racially?), she has rightly pointed to race as a crucial interpretive framework for understanding how violence is legitimized and the central place that cultural attitudes toward different bodies occupy in histories of religious violence.

---

18 Christopher MacEvitt, *The Crusades and the Christian World of the East: Rough Tolerance* (Philadelphia: University of Pennsylvania Press, 2008).

19 Geraldine Heng, *The Invention of Race in the European Middle Ages* (Cambridge: Cambridge University Press, 2018), 123.

From the point of view of exploring crusade violence, Heng's work reminds us that much is at stake in how we choose to view such violence and that understanding the vocabularies of discrimination and violence is both historical and critical practice. If we follow only the medieval polemical texts which sometimes justified violence along confessional lines, we risk replicating their taxonomies. And this is not the end point of any analysis of violence but perhaps only its start. What Heng has usefully done is to draw attention to the somatic elements of medieval anthropologies and their interplay with social and cultural attitudes expressed in textual and ritual form. The lens of "race" is one way of thinking through that interplay. Importantly, too, considering how categories of historical analysis have themselves shaped our assumptions about the past helps to lead us away from the argument that medieval violence was primarily about hostility to religious difference.

This latter point is especially pressing given that, in recent times, a popular idea that the crusades were a "clash of civilizations" has continued to maintain traction in some quarters. This view, articulated by Bernard Lewis and then elaborated into a large-scale theory of global politics by Samuel Huntington, has been the subject of critique by academics for some time not least because it polarizes Christianity and Islam in service of a particular and problematic vision of "the West" as a political, cultural, and religious entity. At the same time, this rhetoric assumes that all crusaders participating in every crusade shared the same view that they were fighting against "Islam." There is no doubt that hostility toward Muslim groups existed, as is clear from the examples I have presented above. But the idea that crusaders were motivated to conduct these holy wars solely on the basis of religious difference is not the case. And explaining crusade violence as a monolithic and one-dimensional struggle between Christianity and Islam is not only superficial but also, as we have seen with the co-opting of such rhetoric by right-wing extremists to justify their own violence, dangerous. This being the case then, looking at violence against groups who were represented in polemical texts as hostile, unjustly occupying holy spaces, and legitimate targets, also necessitates looking at the underlying principles of crusading and the place of individual crusaders in the work of holy war.

Instruments of Violence

The corporeal turn in history asks us to consider all bodies, not just bodies that are clearly physically and rhetorically excluded from societies and cultures. This is important for exploring crusade violence, given that each crusader's own corporeality was itself an instrument and receptacle of violence. Certainly, the cultural and religious projects of "othering" and scapegoating were intended to identify some bodies as deserving of punitive, zealous, and protective exercises of violence. But violence was not hermeneutically limited to physical or rhetorical force against "the other." The crusader's own body was represented as an important site of legitimate violence and an important instrument of violence. Reflecting on how violence generated cultural meaning beyond conflict between polarized groups helps us to understand both the embeddedness of violence in crusade discourse, its complexity, and its relationship with wider spiritual contexts and practices.

Medieval crusade narratives saw individual bodily suffering as an integral part of a crusader's interior and pious motivation for engaging in holy war right from the start. One example may be seen in the *Gesta Francorum*'s representation of Pope Urban II's Clermont sermon, where the Pope is represented as preaching: "Brethren, we ought to endure much suffering for the name of Christ—misery, poverty, nakedness, persecution, want, illness, hunger, thirst, and other (ills) of this kind, just as the Lord saith to His disciples: 'Ye must suffer much in My name'..." (chapter 1). The *Gesta* also emphasizes the significant suffering undergone by the crusaders during the crusade journey itself, especially during the siege and capture of Antioch, representing this moment as a particularly difficult test for the armies before capturing Jerusalem. This is mirrored in other early crusade narratives which, as Andrew Buck has outlined, also described the battle for Antioch as a sort of pious test of endurance. For Robert the Monk, Antioch was a test for the faithful "through the constant pressures of your enemies," while for Fulcher of Chartres, the suffering at Antioch was a means of cleansing crusader sin through "the trial of your faith."[20] Later crusade calls continued to stress the need for violence done to the crusader's own body as part of the spiritual exercise of crusading. The anonymous *Ordinacio de predicacione S. Crucis*, composed in England sometime after 1216 for the use of crusade preachers, included material recommended for use in recruitment sermons including exempla, or moral stories. One of these told the story of a crusader who, in the midst of battle, was near-fatally wounded in four places, but (against the advice of a doctor) wanted to go back into combat to procure a fifth wound like Christ. This he did, killing many Saracens in the meantime.[21]

Suffering in Christ's name meant mirroring Christ's own sacrifice. This was not only understood as the sort of pious endurance we find in the above-mentioned crusade narratives. But, as Susannah Throop has recently made clear in her chapter on crusading violence, it also meant imitating Christ's "victory over sin and death on the cross"—Christ's own redemptive fight.[22] This drew together suffering and fighting; imitating Christ involved individual physical suffering *and* military action. The crusader's own body was the site at which these components of crusading violence were located. The mimetic aspects of crusading were not universal; the Cistercian preaching of the Second Crusade did not centre this motif, for example. But imitation of Christ certainly grew stronger from the later twelfth

20 Andrew Buck, "'Weighed by Such a Great Calamity, They Were Cleansed for Their Sins': Remembering the Siege and Capture of Antioch," in *Remembering the Crusades in Medieval Texts and Songs*, ed. Buck and Smith (Cardiff: University of Wales Press, 2019), 2–7.

21 Christoph Maier, "*Brevis ordinacio de Predicacione Sancte Crucis*: Edition, Translation and Commentary," *Crusades* 18 (2019): 25–65.

22 Throop, "Not Cruelty but Piety," 418.

century and became emphatic during the thirteenth-century crusades. The Franciscan scholar Gilbert of Tournai's mid-thirteenth century sermon to those who were preparing to take up the cross told crusaders that they not only carried "this cross of Christ in your heart," but they carried "his stigmata on your body so that, offering the sacrifice of a burnt offering inside, you have his skin on the outside."[23] Here, the act of fighting and dying for Christ is understood to use the crusader's body to imitate Christ's own suffering and death. At the same time, Gilbert reminded crusaders that their suffering "is little, indeed nothing, compared to the immeasurable reward… the sufferings of this present time are nothing compared to the future glory which will be disclosed for us."[24] As a troubadour of the mid-thirteenth century sang, "he who strews his brains, or his blood or his innards, on the soil of the land where God was born of his handmaiden, will have a lofty seat before God in Paradise."[25]

The combined activities of fighting and imitation of Christ were drawn together institutionally in the Knights Templar whose variety of "muscular Christianity" was played out in their unique status as warriors/monks/pilgrims. These were *milites* who were also ascetics, regulating their bodies in the service of Christ as did other medieval religious, but instrumentalizing that asceticized body in the practice of violence. As the Anglo-Norman historian Orderic Vitalis commented, the Templars were admirable because they "devote their lives to the bodily and spiritual service of God and rejecting all the things of this world, face martyrdom daily."[26] And the act of embodying imitation of Christ was manifested individually and materially through the practice among some early crusaders of cutting or branding their own bodies with the sign of the

---

23 Christoph Maier, *Crusade Propaganda and Ideology: Model Sermons for the Preaching of the Cross* (Cambridge: Cambridge University Press, 2000), 185.

24 Maier, *Crusade Propaganda and Ideology*, 210.

25 Jackson, *The Seventh Crusade*, 19.

26 Orderic Vitalis, *Historia Ecclesiastica*, ed. Chibnall, 6:310–11.

cross. William Purkis has outlined how this practice—making flesh bleed and permanently tattooing the skin—was an especially overt means of showing "Christo-mimetic self-mortification" and its relationship to becoming a crusader.[27]

The nature of crusade suffering was not unchanging, particularly as participation in crusading expanded over time and crusading privileges came to be extended to non-combatants. Pope Clement III, for example, had extended Holy Land privileges to Spain in 1188. This meant that indulgences were granted to non-combatants who had made a material contribution to the ongoing set of conflicts in the Iberian Peninsula, and that crusades in Spain were of equivalent merit to those in the Holy Land. This particular extension of privileges was retracted by Pope Innocent III in 1213 in order to focus crusading military effort on the new crusade to the Holy Land set in motion by *Quia Maior*. Yet at the same time, from Innocent's pontificate onwards, participation in crusading widened and included material donation and spiritual work on the home front. Anne Lester's work on the spiritual efforts of thirteenth-century Cistercian nuns in northern France showed clearly the connections between penitential piety and crusading. For women in the convents of Champagne, suffering meant sharing the imitation of Christ with male crusaders through care for the poor and sick as well as through renunciation of the world for a prayerful, ascetic life within the convent. The elision, as Lester notes, of crusade piety with its sacrificial and renunciative emphasis and monastic piety created not just a new focus on the place of the suffering body in the work of medieval Christians at this time, but also a new way of imagining how crusading could be undertaken and by whom.[28]

---

27 William J. Purkis, "Zealous Imitation: The Materiality of the Crusader's Marked Body," *Material Religion* 14, no. 4 (2019), 438–53 at 453.

28 Anne E. Lester, "A Shared Imitation: Cistercian Convents and Crusader Families in Thirteenth-Century Champagne," *Journal of Medieval History* 35, no. 4 (2009): 353–70.

During Pope Gregory IX's pontificate, crusading participation expanded further. In the bull *Rachel suum videns* (1234) which was issued to support the preaching of a crusade on the expiry of the truce between Gregory and Holy Roman Emperor Frederick II, the pope used the figure of Rachel to appeal to all sorts of participants in the crusade, including women. Suffering also appears in this crusade call, first in the description of the grief-stricken Rachel at the outset, and then in the request to "die for the sake of life, to endure hardships and disagreeable things" as part of the crusade. As I outlined previously in this book, the biblical figure of Rachel was used to generate collective outrage over the "pollution" of Jerusalem by its unjust invaders. Rachel was also used here to suggest the participation of non-combatants in the crusade. A figure usually associated with the contemplative life (and contrasted with the figure of Leah, her sister, representing the active life), Rachel was mobilized to show that "all who truly undertake this labour with contrite heart and oral confession...according to the quantity of aid and the state of their devotion" may be granted the indulgence.[29] The supportive activities of prayer, procession, financial aid, participation in liturgies, and so on, involved those with the right intent in the practice of crusading, including its suffering, and its concomitant reward.

Violence done to the crusader's body was also part of a discourse of martyrdom that was present (although inconsistently) in many crusade narratives. Early crusade preaching had included the prospect of martyrdom for those who took up the cross, while once the potential conversion of Muslims came to be included in some thirteenth-century crusade calls, a desire for martyrdom was enfolded into mendicant activities in north Africa and missions to the Mongols. The possibility of martyrdom was expressed by the French king Louis IX who is said to have inspired his troops before battle in 1248 by reminding them that "For us, every outcome means deliverance: if we are defeated, we fly forth as martyrs; if we are

---

29 Bird, Peters, and Powell, eds., *Crusade and Christendom*, 270–76.

victorious, the glory of God will be proclaimed and that of all France—indeed of Christendom—will be enhanced."[30] Louis IX, whose own body was represented by his biographers as virile and robust but then stricken by disease and weakened prior to his death on crusade in 1270, reminded his followers of both the reward of crusading and the centrality of the body in gaining that reward. Martyrdom depended on violence, the more graphic the better, such as the tale, recorded in an exemplum by the thirteenth-century Dominican Stephen of Bourbon (based on a tale in the early twelfth-century *Historia Hierosolymitana* of Peter Tudebode), of a knight captured during the siege of Antioch who was led onto the city walls by his captors and instructed to dissuade the crusaders from their attack. He refused and was decapitated by his captors and as they were about to toss his severed head from the city walls were startled by it laughing at them, signifying the knight's salvation.[31]

Finally, crusaders inhabited a world enlivened by everyday and multivalent encounters with bodily fragmentation. The collection and circulation of relics, sacred items associated with holy people, events, or sites, included body parts, while the developing theology of the resurrection of the body invited reflection on the meaning of fragmentation and redemption. Relics were precious spiritual, economic, and social objects which influenced pilgrimage practices and brought prestige to the specific locations that housed them. The body parts venerated by medieval pilgrims and others were themselves communicative devices, conduits to the sacred, the means by which saints themselves were remembered and petitioned. In war contexts, fragmented bodies could also "speak," perhaps not overtly like the laughing head described by Stephen of Bourbon, but more often as narrative devices in reports of the efficacious suffering borne

30 Jackson, *The Seventh Crusade*, 87.

31 Etienne de Bourbon, *Anecdotes historiques. Légendes et Apologues*, ed. A. Lecoy de la Marche (Paris: Société de l'histoire de France, 1877), 91.

by crusaders. When Walter the Chancellor's *Bella Antio-chena* (ca. 1115–1122) told of injured crusaders who "fell at the hands of the heathen not only with their heads cut off but [suffering] agonising death with the skin flayed from the living and half-severed head," he wanted both to stress the brutality of their executioners and to illustrate the tremendous sacrifice of the crusaders.[32] The frequency of reports of decapitation in early crusade narratives is striking, too. Often described in the context of the poor treatment of captives, the beheading of crusaders was meant to suggest the trials of the martyrs, reinforce the notion of an excessively cruel enemy, and generate horror and anger among Christians who might then take up the cross themselves.

Yet bodily dismemberment, including decapitation, was perhaps even more frequently reported as an element of crusader violence itself. Sometimes this was a military tactic of intimidation, such as the *Gesta Francorum*'s reports that "our men hurled the heads of the killed far into the city of Nicaea, so that they (the Turks) might be the more terrified thereafter" (chapter 8), or the report that "[the crusaders] carried the heads of one hundred dead before the gate of the city, where the envoys of the Emir of Babylon, who had been sent to the princes, were encamped" (chapter 11). These heads of executed Turks were trophies of war, according to Anselm of Ribemont, lord of Ostremont and Valenciennes, who wrote to archbishop Manasses II of Reims during the First Crusade, reporting that after the successful siege of Nicaea: "our men, moreover, returning in victory and bearing many heads fixed on pikes and spears, furnished a joyful spectacle for the people of God."[33] These sorts of images are commonly replicated in the visual culture of crusading, especially in manuscript images of the thirteenth century. Manuscripts such as Paris

---

32 *Walter the Chancellor's Antiochene Wars: A Translation*, trans. Thomas S. Asbridge and Susan B. Edgington (Burlington: Ashgate, 1999), 132.

33 Dana Carleton Munro, ed., *Letters of the Crusaders*, rev. ed. (Philadelphia: University of Pennsylvania, 1902), 3.

Bibliothèque nationale de France (BnF), fr. 2630 (folio 22v from northern France ca. 1275) shows decapitated enemy heads being hurled into the city of Nicaea, or Boulogne-sur-Mer, Bibliothèque municipale (BM), MS 142, folio 49v (from St Jean d'Acre, ca. 1280s) which contains an image of an inhabitant of Antioch being beheaded by a crusader. In the context of violence, the military reality of dismemberment as a result of sword combat is only one reason why the imagery of decapitation was included in narratives. Bodily dismemberment was part of a wider cultural economy of actions and symbols that communicated justice, punishment, power and hierarchy—"the climax of myriad conflicts"—that communicated the history and memory of crusading violence.[34]

Conclusion

I have suggested here that the treatment of bodies and the representations of bodies to whom violence might be directed formed part of a distinctive culture of crusading violence. The construction of certain bodies as deserving of violence was meant to communicate that these bodies needed to be contained, punished, or prevented from polluting Christendom. The graphic depictions of bodily violence we see in narratives are therefore part of a behavioural culture that also brought together suffering, vengeance, and the legitimization of conflict. Integral to the justification of violence done to the bodies of Jews, Muslims, and others during this period was also the crusader's own body, and—returning to Skoda's argument—the notion that bodily violence was an important communicative device. We cannot be satisfied solely with

---

34 *Heads Will Roll: Decapitation in the Medieval and Early Modern Imagination*, ed. Larissa Tracy and Jeff Massey (Leiden: Brill, 2012), 13. For the manuscript images see: BnF MS fr. 2630, fol. 22v: https://commons.wikimedia.org/wiki/Category:Bibliothèqu e_Nationale,_Paris,_MS_Fr_2630#/media/File:CrusadersThrowing HeadsOfMuslimsOverRamparts.jpg; and Boulogne-sur-Mer, BM MS 142, fol. 49v: https://bvmm.irht.cnrs.fr/iiif/114/canvas/ canvas-94335/view.

arguments about "othering" to explain the choice to commit crusading violence; doing so captures only one part of what I understand to be a corporeal set of communicative actions with a range of meanings and intents.

Crusading violence also contained a distinctive temporality and apocalypticism—the idea that the end times as prophesized in the Bible were imminent—was an important strand of both crusade preaching and action. Some thought that they were setting in motion the events that would lead to the final battle and Christ's second coming by means of participating in the crusade. These tied violence to a more transcendent medieval narrative about God's eternal scheme and the place of crusading within it. In this narrative, violence was not just part of an earthly military conflict, but was also thought to be part of foreordained eschatological history and the means by which that history was activated. These complex temporal dimensions of crusading were also tied to memory; the memory of Christ's Passion, the memory of biblical exemplars and prophecy, and increasingly, the memory of previous crusades. The next chapter of this book will track the connections between violence and memory a little more closely.

Chapter 3

Memories, Emotions, and Aftermaths of Violence

The aim of this book has been to explore medieval under-standings of crusade violence and consider some of the contexts in which violence was justified or condemned. We have seen how violence emerged from a range of contexts, was expressed in diverse vocabularies communicated in text, preaching, song, and was played out in material and imagined settings. I have tried to illustrate how crusading violence was rhetorical and performative but also real and experienced. My focus so far has been on crusaders them-selves and the environments which informed their thinking and action. In this chapter, I want to shift this focus to con-sider how violence was remembered during and after the crusades. I'm focussing here on the emotional dimensions of memory, the performance of memory in medieval crusade culture, and contemporary (i.e., post-medieval) memories of crusade violence.

Understanding how violence is remembered is a crucial aspect of understanding violence itself, given that violence attaches itself to memory in all sorts of ways. Many modern studies of war have shown that victims of war may experi-ence the disruption of memory, the inability to relegate a violent event to the past, the constant intrusion of memories of violence into present consciousness. In modern medical discourse, this is "trauma"—a constant replaying of a violent experience that prevents that event from being psychologi-cally consigned to "the past." Memory of violence may also be more positively marshalled into the service of testimony and witnessing. Again, the many modern studies of the aftermath of events marked by atrocity such as the Holocaust, the apartheid era in South Africa, the genocides in Rwanda and Cambodia, among many others, have shown how bringing to light memories of experienced violence is necessary for prosecutions or truth and reconciliation processes, and also for historicization—the testimonial and ethical work of "never forgetting" in order to build a different future.

At the same time, we know that remembering violence might also be actively celebrated in cultural memory, becoming part of how groups imagine their collective identities and shape national stories. Sometimes this kind of work of memory is ritualized and performed (remembrance services, veterans' days) and sometimes it is materialized (monuments and memorials). In medieval contexts, crusading was a memorial culture in a range of social ways, too. Crusaders memorialized their own and their family experiences through participation in liturgical practices, connection with religious houses, collecting and circulating memory objects, and the production of written texts such as narrative histories. These many cultural forms of remembering remind us that memory is as much a social practice as it is an individual, interior inclination. Remembering is embedded in social and cultural conceptions of belonging, participation and, as Nicholas Paul and others have shown, medieval identity formation.

In this chapter, I want to look at these two aspects of crusading violence to think about how crusade violence was remembered and accommodated in both medieval and postmedieval cultures. Where are traces of memory? How do we set about finding them? What is the place of violence in contemporary cultural memories of the crusades?

Emotion

Crusade violence was not just physical. It was also experienced psychologically or mentally, and expressed in many crusade sources by what we might describe as the language of emotion. Over the last decade or so, the history of emotions has been illuminated by numerous studies which together have shown that emotion is a rich category of social and cultural analysis and that emotions were used in past societies for many purposes, all of which should be contextually situated. Rosenwein's notion that communities formed and were expressed by common understanding and performance of emotions has been one especially influential framework in medieval history. Historians of the crusades, too, have more recently come to consider the place and importance of emotions. Stephen Spencer's pioneering work explored the rhetoric of emotions in a broad range of crusade texts, showing that emotion words and language did not necessarily represent the lived reality of crusade experience, but rather was carefully deployed to reinforce particular ideas about the nature of the holy war and its participants.[35]

Spencer's work revealed the deliberate inclusion of emotion in crusade sources, the historical moments when emotions seem to have become especially important to use in those texts, and the continual presence of emotional representation across the crusading period. Spencer's observations are also pertinent to how we might approach the memory of crusade violence. This is for two principal reasons. First, memory, like emotion, is not only individual and cognitive but also socio-cultural and performative. So, methodological borrowings from the history of emotions may help to navigate the similarly interior/exterior features of memory too. Second, emotions were a significant feature of the language of remembrance in medieval texts. Violent experiences were often expressed in emotional terms by those who reported it, using widely understood emotion words and themes. This was true for both the victims of violence and those who committed violence even though the cultural scripts informing

35 Barbara Rosenwein, *Emotional Communities in the Early Middle Ages* (Ithaca: Cornell University Press, 2006); Stephen J. Spencer, *Emotions in a Crusading Context, 1095-1291* (Oxford: Oxford University Press, 2019).

such reports/representations differed across culture, time and place, as did the audience to whom those representations were directed.

Muslim reactions to the presence of crusaders in the Holy Land provide one example of how emotion and memory worked together. These reactions were various and involved military responses, pleas for help and calls for unification and explanations for the events, while Carole Hillenbrand sets these initial reactions in the context of general alarming signs including astrological and the plague that happened in Egypt in 1097 and 1099–1100—an overall psychological "atmosphere of gloom" which included religious schisms dividing the Muslim world. The earliest texts to reflect on the First Crusade used emotional language to inform and motivate Muslims against this general background of political, religious, and cosmological upheaval. One of the earliest of these surviving responses is the *Kitab al-Jihad* by al-Sulami, composed in 1105 as a sermon for the mosque at Damascus.[36] Al-Sulami asks his listeners to strive for the good of their souls in order to strive for the defeat of the enemy. The internal *jihad*, or struggle, in other words, is the priority. Reflecting on the "killing, capture, torture, and torment" inflicted by the invaders, al-Sulami reminds Muslims that collective and unified action is necessary, but that success can only come with obedience to God. Humiliation, shame, and disgrace are the emotional outcomes of inaction and fear, while the translation of inner devotion and obedience to outward action will bring "liberation in this world from the shame." In this sermon the memory of the crusade's very recent violence is used to spark another form of remembering; that is, the reminder that obedience to God is fundamental to all action, both spiritual and physical.

The idea of a movement of inner feeling to outward action appears in other early reactions to the crusade. Weeping is

---

36 Extracts from the *Book of the Jihad* of Ali Ibn Tahir Al-Sulami, in Niall Christie, *Muslims and Crusaders: Christianity's Wars in the Middle East, 1095–1382, from the Islamic Sources* (London: Routledge, 2014), 133–35.

a feature of a poem by al-Abiwardi (d. 1113) who conflated blood and tears in his commentary on the First Crusade: "we have mixed blood with flowing tears and there are none of us left worth pitying/ the tears that a man sheds are the worst of weapons when sharp blades stir up the fires of war," he wrote in a poem designed to motivate "brave Arabs" to avoid disgrace and dishonour by engaging in war.[37] The emphasis on war to avenge dishonour also evokes fear to motivate Muslims to take up arms. This is sometimes expressed in terms of the number of invading Franks—"the polytheists have swollen in a flood of which the torrent [of the sea] is frightened by the extent," "armies like mountains have stormed out of the land of the *Ifranja* to bring about our destruction" (Ibn al-Khayyat, d. 1120s)—and sometimes it is expressed by the threat that the invaders pose to women and girls—"children's hair turns white [with fear]" (al-Abiwardi), "mothers of young girls...are almost wasting away with fear" (al-Khayyat). The use of these sorts of motifs are intended to remind Muslims of both their pious and social obligations to respond to the crusaders. As scholars have long noted, these reactions and exhortations were critiques of Muslim disunity and sinfulness, both of which were thought by medieval Muslims to have enabled crusader success.

Once the early crusades enter into the realm of cultural memory through the act of historical writing, representations of violence obtain slightly different dimensions. Although the chronicle of Ibn Al-Athir (completed around 1230) portrays the 1099 capture of Jerusalem as an episode "which brought tears to the eye and pained the heart," there develops a perhaps unsurprising triumphalist tone to some other episodes. Imad al-Din al-Isfahani (d. 1201), for instance, includes a striking description of the aftermath of the battle of Hattin in 1187 where the dismembered bodies of dead Franks, "heads cracked open, throats split, spines broken, necks shattered, feet in pieces, noses mutilated, extremities torn off..." were strewn across the plain as a "lesson to the wise." Imad al-Din

---

37 Christie, *Muslims and Crusaders*, 130.

wrote a similarly florid and extremely distressing account of the rape of Christian women after Saladin's capture of Jerusalem—"bringing a smile to Muslim faces at their lamentations"—setting this episode in the context of the purification of the city, vengeance, and righteous justice.[38] Imad al-Din was in the service of Saladin at this time, and his writing was characteristic of the prose style of chancery documents with which he was familiar as a *kātib*, or secretary. This elaborate style was to be read for its symbolic and propaganda value while elevating Saladin's legacy.[39] Saladin's triumph at Hattin and Jerusalem provided Imad al-Din with ample opportunity to use violence in the service of memory through heightened, emotion-driven prose.

The profound disruption to memory that modern analysts describe as trauma has been recently used to understand the impact of crusade violence, including on crusaders themselves. As noted above, trauma signifies not only a profound ontological and psychological shock caused by an experience or event, but a collapse of memory and time that results in the inability to put something in the past, so the experience is always and intrusively present. Historians who have used trauma as a category of historical analysis have shown how remembering is individually and collectively central to the narration of a traumatic event. In particular, what we call the "recursive impulse" of trauma—the replaying of the experience over and over—and its connection with the formation of cultural memory has opened up new ways of thinking about reactions to violence by those who experienced it in different times and places. We can see this sort of replaying at work, for instance, in crusade calls and historical representations

---

38 Both episodes are translated in Francesco Gabrieli, ed. and trans., *Arab Historians of the Crusades*, trans. E. J. Costello (orig. publ. as *Storici Arabi delle Crociate*, Turin: Einaudi, 1957; Berkeley: University of California Press, 1984), 135 and 163.

39 Lutz Richter-Bernburg, "Imad al-Din al Isfahani," in *Medieval Muslim Historians and the Franks in the Levant*, ed. Alex Mallett (Leiden: Brill, 2014), 29–51.

that followed the loss of Jerusalem in 1187 which reiterated emotional tropes and images such as the loss of the True Cross in order to create some sort of meaning around this disastrous event. Well beyond 1187, images of the loss of this precious relic and the city of Jerusalem include similar rhetoric. Looking closely at the language of calls for a crusade is one way that the memory of violence and its impact might thus be traced.

Crusade calls, those sermons and letters generated at the papal curia and designed to encourage Christians to take up the cross, were generally one important means by which the memory of crusade violence was imbued with urgent meaning and expressed in emotional terms. This may be traced in a number of texts, including papal correspondence meant for wide circulation, to stir up enthusiasm for the crusade through preaching. One example is the papal letter *Plorans ploravit*, which I mentioned in the first chapter of this book in the context of gendered language and spaces of violence. This letter was produced in the very active papal curia of Pope Innocent III at the end of June, 1198 and was meant to guide the preaching of the crusade in southern Italy and Sicily. Its relevant broad contexts include both the aftermath of the Third Crusade and the continued loss of Jerusalem and other holy places, and a failed Sicilian crusade of 1197. *Plorans ploravit* represents something of a precursor of the more famous crusade call known as *Post miserabile* which was sent out in August of that year, only a couple of months after *Plorans* was issued.

The most overt emotions in *Plorans ploravit* are (perhaps unsurprisingly) grief and anger. The opening words of the latter, as I previously remarked, are lamentations derived from Matthew 2:18 and Jeremiah 31:15: "Weeping the Church weeps and a voice is heard in Rama of weeping and great lamentation." After reporting the devastations wrought on the Holy Land and its sacred places, the pope refers to Psalm 2:1–2 ("why have the gentiles raged and the people devised vain things? The kings of the earth stood up and the princes met together against the Lord and against his Christ"). Here,

Innocent reiterates the idea that Christian sin has brought about these terrible events, and at particular fault are the divided Christian secular leaders whose anger and dissension—unregulated and misdirected emotion—has led to the parlous situation of the Holy Land. This rebuke was intended to resonate especially with the Sicilian and southern Italian audiences who might hear the themes of the letter in sermon; their ongoing political turmoil was of real concern to this pope. The letter's images and tropes of lamentation and grief were also recently familiar to the medieval audiences familiar with Pope Gregory VIII's crusade call, *Audita tremendi*, a decade prior, which had mourned the loss of Jerusalem, telling Christians that "whoever does not mourn…so great a cause for sorrow…is ignorant…of our very humanity."

Crusade calls like *Plorans ploravit* delineated the sort of anger that was to underpin the exercise of crusade violence. In *Plorans*, anger is both God's anger and the righteous anger that those who hear of the desecration of holy places ought to feel. Innocent is particularly concerned to channel this anger into vengeance: "we have sent letters…so that sons may avenge the injuries of the father, and brothers may arm to avenge their slain brothers." And he is also concerned to communicate both collective and personal or intimate reasons for response. "Who will refuse to die for him, who for our sake was made obedient unto death, death even on the cross?," he wrote. The familial language to which I have referred earlier in this book is also wielded to generate the dutiful and collective response that Innocent hoped for. He refers to the church as mother, to the potential participants as sons.

Post miserabile, the crusade call issued by Pope Innocent III only a matter of months after *Plorans ploravit*, again deploys emotional imagery from Lamentations and various psalms. Words like "wretched," "lamentable," "deplorable," "ignominious," "awful," "agonising," set the tone while grief is dramatically rendered: "the Apostolic See, alarmed at the awful recurrence of disasters so unfortunate, was struck with agonizing grief, exclaiming and bewailing to such a degree that, from her continual crying, her throat became hoarse [Ps 68:4]. And from excessive weeping, her eyes became dim."[40] The griev-ous damage done to holy places is narrated (profanation of the holy sepulchre) and is particularly attached to the idea that Christ has been injured and these injuries—bodily and spatial—must be avenged by means of the instrument of holy war. The crusade is also meant to "rebut the scorn" of the "insulters" (i.e., Muslims) who have witnessed the moral shortcomings of the Christian princes to ask "where is your God" and to taunt western Christians with the possession of holy places and continued military defeats. For Innocent, these insults should spur action to aid the Holy Land, and they should generate emotions of anger and vengeance in defence of what he understood to be Christ's patrimony.

These interior emotions of future crusaders are overt in *Post miserabile*, not just in terms of reaction to the state of the Holy Land, but also in terms of the right motivation for undertaking the crusade. The right feelings are important for all those who are to participate in the crusade effort: for those who fight, humility is stressed. And for those who support from the home-front, strength of devotion is rewarded: "we also state that all persons who shall give suitable aid to the Holy Land at their own cost, according to the amount of aid they give, and especially in proportion to the depth of devo-tion they shall manifest, shall be partakers in this remission." So, the emotional act or "depth of devotion" qualified a per-son for remission of sins. Likewise, potential crusaders should not feel pride for any successes they might realize. Innocent warns them that "If you set out upon your pilgrimage with all humility of heart and body, as you ought to do, the Lord may effect that which he did not grant to your forefathers. Proba-bly, our forefathers might have conspired together and would have said, 'our own high hand and not the Lord has done all this'" (quoting Deuteronomy 32:27). Thus, Pope Innocent III both laid out an emotional register for his promotion of the crusade and violence early on, and fused emotion, memory, and violence in his call to arms. This was in the language of

---

40 Bird, Peters, and Powell, *Crusade and Christendom*, 31.

his letters but also in the agenda of getting secular leaders to reconcile, stop fighting—to regulate their emotions and direct them appropriately and militarily in the service of God.

Performative Memory

Collective Christian actions beyond the battlefront thus helped to promote the idea that all Christendom should be united in the prosecution of the holy war. This ambition was especially apparent in the liturgical activities—prayers, masses, and alms—that were practised in the west and in the Holy Land from the preaching of the First Crusade. Liturgies were often collective and public ritual performances involving both prayer and procession and formed part of the sacred rhythm of daily life for medieval Christians. They were important expressions of common ideas and communal effort and specific crusade liturgies, described by Pope Honorius III as "invisible weapons," were important ways in which the prayerful effort of Christians beyond the battlefield could (it was hoped) direct the outcome of military events. From the earliest crusades, liturgy was enfolded into crusading practice through rites for taking up the cross and rites for departure, while the development of collective liturgical efforts on behalf of crusaders and crusades became common thereafter.

As M. Cecilia Gaposchkin has shown, crusade liturgies were also acts of memory. The celebration of the capture of Jerusalem in 1099 was commemorated in liturgical form on July 15 and even inscribed on the liturgical calendars of the same monastic houses that also produced narratives of the crusade. Singing the words of violence—for instance, "the pavement of the temple is made bloody with the blood of those who are dying"—integrated the memory of crusade violence into the ritual activity of Christian life.[41] Liturgical activity could likewise memorialize crusade disasters more generally in order to mobilize support for new crusading

---

41 M. Cecilia Gaposchkin, *Invisible Weapons: Liturgy and the Making of Crusade Ideology* (Ithaca: Cornell University Press, 2017).

efforts: after the loss of Jerusalem in 1187 Pope Clement III ordered that special prayers be offered in all Christian churches asking God for assistance in retaking the city. By 1150, when the situation in the Holy Land was quite different and the Second Crusade had (in 1148) failed, the character of the liturgy had significantly altered too. Two commemorative services were now included: one to honour the crusaders who had died in the First Crusade and one to honour Godfrey of Bouillon. Even more change occurred after the loss of Jerusalem in 1187. After this disaster, prayers for the release of crusader captives were introduced into the liturgy, for example. And by 1250, the commemorative tone of the liturgy was unsurprisingly lament, rather than celebration. As historians of crusade liturgy have observed, if there had been an early shift towards liturgical remembrance of individual or collective heroic crusaders, after the disaster of Al-Mansurah which brought to an end King Louis IX's crusade in 1250, the liturgy became a mode of collective mourning, as processions now passed through graveyards.[42] Liturgical activities thus collapsed sacred and contemporary time in acts of remembrance which were both spiritual and martial. Widespread crusade liturgies also meant that sacred violence was normalized in the regular ritual remembrances of all western Christians. Such actions helped to expand crusade activity beyond the confines of the battlefield, shaping communities of performative memory throughout Christendom, and using the vehicle of common liturgies to draw all Christians together in prayerful recollection.[43]

Crusading was also remembered in material form, on both large and small scale. There are many examples of land grants to monastic houses (especially the military orders) by those who were either about to depart on crusade or who were grateful for their safe return, or by the families of dead

---

42 Schein, *Gateway to the Heavenly City*, 29–31.

43 For the idea of Christendom, see Brett Whalen, *Dominion of God: Christendom and Apocalypse in the Middle Ages* (Cambridge, MA: Harvard Unversity Press, 2009).

crusaders eager to commemorate their actions. Examples of the former in England include the foundation of the Cistercian house of Vale Royal in 1270 by the Lord Edward on the eve of his departure on crusade, or the foundation of the Carmelite house of Hulne in England by a returning crusader in 1240 who had been reminded of Mount Carmel by the elevated location at Hulne. Medieval cultures of crusade memory were also smaller in scale and highly mobile. The best example here is of the collection and circulation of relics which travelled with crusaders on their journeys or were collected by them on campaign. The relics associated with Christ himself, particularly relics of the Passion, were commonly gifted, translated, or sold, such as the holy blood relic given to Hailes abbey in 1270 by the earl of Cornwall, or the many relics of the True Cross which formed a central part of the sacred collections of monasteries and churches. Even stones from the church of the Holy Sepulchre or dust from the Holy Land circulated in the west and travelled with crusaders as they went on their journeys, while other small precious items such as rings were bought or commissioned while crusaders were travelling and subsequently entered family collections. As Nicholas Paul has shown, these sorts of objects became heirlooms, creating family memories and genealogical narratives about participation in and support for holy war. More practical military items such as armour or swords were left in wills and sometimes reused, connecting crusaders across generations and campaigns.[44] These objects were sometimes specifically embellished with the identifying features of a family and crusading. One example is the sword pommel of Pierre de Dreux, Count of Brittany, who accompanied King Louis IX of France on his crusade to Egypt in 1248. The pommel (the decorative top of the sword handle) featured the arms of Pierre de Dreux on one side, and the crusader's cross on the other. Pierre himself was captured during the battle

44 Nicholas Paul, *To Follow in Their Footsteps: The Crusades and Family Memory in the High Middle Ages* (Ithaca: Cornell University Press, 2012).

of Mansourah in 1250 and held for ransom along with Louis IX. His sword, only the pommel of which now survives in New York's Metropolitan Museum of Art, formed a visual part of the memory of his own aristocratic crusading identity and his family's connection to it.

It is worth noting that custodians of crusade memory were also often women, who sometimes faced very different lives once husbands and family members departed for a crusade. Although it is not possible to quantify how many women were left widowed as a result of their husband's deaths on crusade, various legal and administrative sources such as charters and wills hint at ways in which women's lives were changed as a result of their husband's deaths. Helisent of Joigny was one war widow who sold off her whole dowry and entered a convent when her husband and son were killed on the Fifth Crusade. Others found themselves holding large estates, sometimes pressed into remarriage, and sometimes ably remaining single. Professed religious women were frequently petitioned to say special prayers for absent or departed crusaders, and their convents were the repositories of memory for the families of crusaders. The Cistercian convents of northern France were particularly favoured by crusaders, as the nuns were thought to mirror the sacrificial suffering of the crusaders themselves. Crusaders left their bodies to be buried at Cistercian nunneries, like Hugh de Chatillon who died in 1248 and was interred at the nunnery of Pont-aux-Dames. Likewise Raoul II of Courcy, who died at Al-Mansurah the same year and whose remains were returned to the Cistercian house of Longpont to be buried with the rest of his family.[45]

Other communities created and experienced their own memories of violence through visual cultures which connected biblical models, crusade conflicts, and collective remembrance in various ways. One example is the fictitious duel between Richard I of England and Saladin, which was used in religious and royal settings. The well-known floor tiles of the abbeys of Chertsey, Neath, Tintern, and Glastonbury all had

---

45 Lester, "A Shared Imitation."

images of the Saladin/Richard duel, and the same image was also commissioned in the royal context of the Antioch Chamber at Clarendon, which was commissioned by King Henry III of England in 1250.[46] Crusading imagery was also employed by King Edward I of England who commissioned murals for the painted chamber at the palace of Westminster in 1292. These murals depicted Old Testament scenes of the defence of the Holy Land and the life of Judas Maccabeus. These sorts of images were carefully chosen, illustrating biblical connections to royal crusading and also heroic, epic stories. Chief among the themes of such images, whether biblical or heroic, is the violence of combat itself, which was intended to associate individual monarchs with actual military prestige.

The same sort of emphasis on violence is also found in the rich visual culture of manuscript illumination depicting crusade events. Images of events such as those of the siege of Nicaea and the siege of Antioch during the First Crusade were depicted in illustrated copies of William of Tyre's well-circulated *Historia* (and its vernacular versions) with, as noted in the previous chapter, decapitated enemy heads being hurled into cities (BnF MS fr. 2630, fol. 22v), bleeding enemy corpses piled in the ground (BnF MS fr. 9083, fol. 45r), and the slaughter of citizens within the city walls (Boulogne-sur-Mer BM MS 142, fol. 49v).[47] In the very well-known image of the battle of Hattin that appears in the mid-thirteenth century English *Chronica majora* of Matthew Paris depicts a tussle between the king of Jerusalem (Gui of Lusignan) and Saladin himself over the relic of the True Cross. In this image, the cross is the focal point of a story of violence done to Christ and underscored by the depiction of dismembered corpses of soldiers

---

46 A recent study and reconstruction of the Chertsey tiles is by Amanda Luyster, "Fragmented Tile, Fragmented Text: Richard the Lionheart on Crusade and the Lost Latin Texts of the Chertsey Combat Tiles (c. 1250)," *Digital Philology* 11, no. 1 (2022): 86–120.

47 https://gallica.bnf.fr/ark:/12148/btv1b9006994b/f25.item; https://gallica.bnf.fr/ark:/12148/btv1b90632099/f60.item; https://bvmm.irht.cnrs.fr/iiif/114/canvas/canvas-94335/view.

at the bottom of the image being trampled underfoot by horses. This particular image, part of the manuscript now held in Cambridge, Corpus Christi College (MS 26, fol. 140r) encapsulates nicely in this scene the power of images, the materiality of crusade objects, and the ongoing memory of the loss of the relic well into the thirteenth century.

The Long Memory of Crusade Violence

In this book, I have so far tried to sketch out how the exercise of crusade violence in its diverse forms was continuously thought about and expressed across the twelfth and thirteenth centuries. The logics that underpinned crusader violence were not only built on just/holy war theories but were created in many cultural contexts and imbued with a variety of meanings by different groups. There was not a singular "form" or even expression of crusade violence—even though some polemicists asserted it was so. Violence was imagined, rehearsed, represented by participants in and targets of crusading in many ways, implicitly and explicitly. This means that there are different approaches one might take in understanding how crusade violence was envisaged and worked. Here, I have concentrated on space, the body, emotion and memory as avenues into historical understanding of crusade violence. It is my hope that further scholarly attention to the cultural turn will bring to light new readings of this medieval problem.

This "medieval problem" is, however, also a modern problem. The integration of the idea of the crusade into post-medieval discourses is not something that has only recently occurred, but it is perhaps in contemporary settings that it has become increasingly more troubling as violence has become more central to this form of medievalism. What precisely constitutes "crusade" violence has stretched its boundaries in the twenty-first century. Reaching beyond the connections between crusade violence and memory in the medieval period to consider the long cultural memory of crusading in more recent times helps us to understand why.

A burgeoning field of crusade scholarship over the last decade or so has been "crusade medievalism," an important area which identifies and analyzes the use of crusades and crusading in different post-medieval regional and national contexts.[48] Medievalism, broadly, is a form of cultural memory where the Middle Ages is invoked in all sorts of cultural, social, and political ways, serving sometimes as a form of nostalgia and at other times as historical justification for present actions. As a large literature on medievalism has long shown, this sort of "longing" for a vanished Middle Ages is closely tied to nineteenth-century political projects and their twentieth-century aftermaths. Crusade medievalism was very often an element of imperialist aspiration and its expressions were used to demonstrate long historical links between past and present. There are many well-known instances of this as Horswell, Siberry, and others have shown. Napoleon Bonaparte's conquest of Malta and invasion of Egypt in 1798 was directly linked to crusades according to historian Joseph-François Michaud (1767–1839), whose encyclopaedic and widely circulated *Histoire des croisades* (1812–1822) stated that the leading place of the French in medieval crusading culture was a clear historical precedent for French involvement in the Levant and eastern Mediterranean. German imperial appropriation of crusading might be seen in the famous example of Kaiser Wilhelm II's 1898 visit to Jerusalem, where he rode into the city dressed as a crusader, imagining himself to be part of the lineage of German crusaders including the emperors Frederick I Barbarossa and Frederick II. These sorts of expressions of crusading were tied to imaginative reconstructions of the Middle Ages more generally, and were intended to legitimize imperial structures and their activities by setting them in the context of longer histories.

---

48 A new series of books and edited collections dealing with the memory of the crusades in the modern period, *Engaging the Crusades* (Routledge), edited by Mike Horswell and Jonathan Phillips has grown swiftly to publish seven titles between 2018 and 2022.

In the search for historical connection to current events, the crusades were invoked in various specific colonial projects, too. The religious dimensions of colonialism, which were also framed as "civilizing" missions, included historical imagery to secure lasting physical presence in the region. For example, in the late nineteenth-century Congo, the church became one of the arms of Belgian colonization (along with the state administration and industry) and the work of missionaries co-existed with the state's atrocities against the Congolese population. The missionaries here saw themselves as rescuing the Congolese from the Arab slave-trade, writing of their efforts to fill the landscape—which was already subject to extensive deforestation by the Belgian industrialists in their inexhaustible search for resources—with medieval-style abbeys and churches. Their rhetoric about slave traders was anti-Muslim and some described their work as a new crusade that was supported by the Belgian king Leopold II, who (initially anyhow) was able to garner European sympathy for his colonization project by linking it to the humanitarian effort to stamp out the slave trade. This "crusade" was supported by a range of devotions in Belgium itself, including the foundation of the Society for Congolese Children in the city of Ghent, where a statue of Our Lady of Congo stood in the chapel of the Trinitarian order, an order founded in 1198 for the redemption of Christian captives enslaved by Muslims during the crusades.

In north Africa, the figure of the French crusader king Louis IX loomed large—literally in Tunisia, where a nineteenth-century statue of the crusade king who had died there in 1270 remains in the historical gardens at Carthage—while in 1830, French troops about to depart for the invasion of Algiers were reminded of their crusading ancestors. Here, the idea of "civilizing barbarians," as it was expressed in many administrative documents, was tied to the historical precedent of war against Muslims in the quest for a new "model colony." In 1920, the French General Henri Gouraud stood before Saladin's grave in the Ummayad mosque in Damascus after the defeat of Arab nationalists and stated "Saladin—

we have returned." The crusade retained significant cultural and political force in these colonization projects as one justification for violent intervention in regions beyond western Europe. The cultural memory of crusading was attached to ideas of western hegemony and entitlement to unfettered territorial expansion.[49]

Crusade medievalisms of the nineteenth and early twentieth centuries were thus connected to bigger ideologies of nation building and the creation of national stories forged in war. Although for the "west," the crusades were essentially a military failure, they became embedded in European national histories nonetheless as nation states invented their origin stories, their myths, and their racial constitutions. In the creation of nation states, and especially those with imperial or colonial ambitions, the crusades came to speak for an imagined past that aligned beautifully with the present. Part of the reason for this was that the crusades always contained a malleable temporality. From their inception the crusades collapsed the present and the past to offer up an eternal future as crusaders imagined themselves as acting in an eschatological story that transcended the earthly realm. In some ways this was also how the historical project itself was conceived of by those nineteenth-century imperialists; a providential and progressive march toward the triumph of western civilization.

The term *hurub al-Salibiya* (wars of the cross, or crusades) came to be used in Arabic from the mid-nineteenth century, notably in the first Arabic history of the crusades written in 1899 by Sayyid Ali Hariri. As many historians have outlined, the fall of the Ottoman empire in 1922 and the subsequent histories of Egypt, Syria, and the eventual survival of the state of Israel from 1948, meant that cultural memories of crusading violence in the Arab world were shaped by contemporary experiences of western presence. Jonathan Phillips has shown that the story of Saladin triumphant was commonly

---

49 Michael Provence, *The Last Ottoman Generation and the Making of the Modern Middle East* (Cambridge: Cambridge University Press, 2017), 3.

invoked in numerous textual and visual cultures to describe both an increasingly inspirational figure and, for some, a historical precedent for dealing with external threats.[50] These threats differed over time, of course, but the use of the historical legacy of the crusades to describe them was, as we have seen in recent times, easily (albeit not inevitably) radicalized in the service of Islamic militancy. Over the course of the twentieth century, jihadism gained new strength, and dichotomies of "us and them"—what Bruce Holsinger called a dualist medievalism of crusade—gained renewed vigour.[51] When isis declared after the Paris massacre of November 2015 that "soldiers of the Caliphate" had targeted the "lead carrier of the cross in Europe" and "cast terror into the hearts of the crusaders in their very own homeland," they echoed the sentiments of Osama bin Laden and others several years earlier who had characterized western Europeans as the descendants of medieval crusaders.[52]

The place of crusade violence, specifically, in such trajectories of cultural memory has, I suggest, become more and more prominent over the last twenty years. In some ways, this is not surprising given that the imperial and colonial projects that invoked historical association with the crusades were fundamentally founded on violence themselves. But in a global environment connected in new digital ways, it is crusade violence specifically that has been increasingly invoked by extremists. In the world of the alt-right, imagined divisions between people based on religion and race are predictably un-nuanced and aggressive. Crusade language is deployed to communicate anti-immigration and anti-Muslim sentiment. Right wing and populist rallies feature a mish-mash of medieval motifs including crusader crosses. In Europe anti-immi-

---

50 Jonathan Phillips, *The Life and Legend of the Sultan Saladin* (London: Bodley Head, 2019).

51 Bruce Holsinger, "Empire, Apocalypse, and the 9/11 Premodern," *Critical Inquiry* 34, no. 3 (2020), 468–90.

52 Jonathan Riley-Smith, *The Crusades, Christianity, and Islam* (New York: Columbia University Press, 2008).

grant gatherings regularly feature wannabe crusaders, who dress in what they think is medieval regalia, carry swords, chant "God wills it/Deus Vult," and refer to the crusades as a real solution to global movements of people. The alt-right in the United States of America and its evangelical arm have embraced a similar mythology. Again, the act of crusading and the medieval era generally provides them with historical solutions to perceived current problems.

But it is violence in particular that characterizes this imaginary white European past for such groups. The man who massacred seventy-seven people in 2011 in Norway thought that the crusades were defensive wars, justified as Christendom was under attack by the Muslim "other" in the Middle Ages. He thought that he was a new Templar, that his murderous rampage was protecting white Europe in the same manner as the original crusaders had done. There is a growing literature by medieval historians on such western appropriations, all of which has shown that at the heart of radical uses of the crusades to justify horrendous actions, lies racism and ideas of white supremacy. Given the connections between idealization of crusading that were forged in the racist enterprises of imperialism and colonization—at the same time that "medieval history" itself was being created as a discipline—current acts of violence are only the most recent manifestation of a trail of modern historical links between violence and the imagined Middle Ages. In a recent volume of essays devoted to tracing these links, we read of crusading imagery in the American ante-bellum south, the Third Reich, and other similarly sobering settings.[53]

I do not mean to imply an unbroken or uniform trajectory of historical thinking from medieval past to modern present that has inevitably resulted in the misuse of the crusades as a model for and justification for violence. The examples and contexts I mention above come with their own histories

---

53 Amy S. Kaufman and Paul B. Sturtevant, *The Devil's Historians: How Modern Extremists Abuse the Medieval Past* (Toronto: University of Toronto Press, 2020).

and complexities. But it is not difficult to trace the creation and development of such thinking given the integration of the idea of the crusade into political, colonial, racist projects over the last centuries, themselves concerned to legitimize violence for various purposes.

Conclusion

Crusade violence itself emerged from and reflected numerous cultural understandings about the legitimacy and illegitimacy of violence, all of which were historically specific. I have suggested that although the philosophical parameters of medieval just/holy war theory certainly give us some insight into the justification for crusade violence, it is in a wider medieval cultural world that we find some answers as to how this played out in practice and what it meant to its participants. Approaching the topic of crusade violence with a cultural turn has, I hope, shown that categories of historical analysis such as space, the body, emotions, and memory offer fruitful insights into crusading mentalities, the many and diverse environments in which thought and action were shaped. It is also important to recognize that ideas about crusading violence were not necessarily static across the entire period of crusading activity. Although there is not space here to track every context in which crusading violence was played out across a long sweep of time and in so many places, I hope that the methodological intervention I have tried to make here will open the way for other studies of crusading violence and historical change.

This book has also sought to show that medieval crusaders did think about violence and its limits. Academic medievalists will not find this to be a revelatory or even startling statement. But time and time again we read of the Middle Ages as a time of unregulated barbarism that can be contrasted with modern civilization. When Steven Pinker wrote as recently as 2011 that "the people of the Middle Ages were gross" and that "medieval Christendom was a culture of cruelty," one could almost hear the howls of despair from medievalists around the globe as yet another characterization of a thousand-year sweep of human history as thoughtlessly violent served to prop up a narrative about the "civilizing process" that replaced it. Central to these sorts of arguments is the implicit (or in Pinker's case explicit) idea that violence was something that was just "done" in the Middle Ages as a matter of course and was not a set of complex and nuanced ideas and actions. In the case of crusade violence, this assumption is simply unfounded. This book has outlined how violence was articulated in text, sermon, song, visual culture, and performance, rehearsed and contested, shaped and received. These were considered and sophisticated genres of cultural communication.

The final section of this book has ended on something of a polemical note, then. This is because understanding violence and how it gathers cultural meaning is important, and not only for historians of the medieval period. The issue of religious violence remains critical in the modern world, so understanding how and why this remains the case necessitates getting history right. Historical practice is based on evidence and argument. History means recognizing and navigating both continuity and change. And to do this work well is an ethical practice. It is history that will help us to understand how the past and present of crusade violence came about; not history as facts that can be arranged as a procession of truths leading to some preordained outcome, but history as practice. The approach we take to engaging with the past will shape the stories that we tell about that past. In the case of crusade violence, we need to attend to all the messy inconsistencies of evidence, the images and metaphors, the many voices that echo from the Middle Ages to tell us something of their world and its worries. It is my hope that this book has helped to move us toward hearing those voices a little more clearly.

Further Reading

The texts below are a snapshot of the some of the more recent English-language work on themes and approaches pertaining to this book.

General

Barber Malcolm. *The New Knighthood: A History of the Order of the Temple*. Cambridge: Cambridge University Press, 1994.

> A still useful introduction to the military orders.

Cole, Penny. *The Preaching of the Crusades to the Holy Land, 1095–1270*. Cambridge, MA: Medieval Academy of America, 1991.

> An important work that details the various themes and sources for crusade preaching across the main period of the crusades.

Constable, Giles. *Crusaders and Crusading in the Twelfth Century*. Farnham: Ashgate, 2008.

> A collection of essays by a significant medievalist and historian of the crusades, including a ground-breaking essay on crusade charters.

Phillips, Jonathan. *The Fourth Crusade and the Sack of Constantinople*. London: Jonathan Cape, 2005.

> A wonderfully readable general history of the controversial Fourth Crusade.

—— . *The Second Crusade: Extending the Frontiers of Christendom*. New Haven: Yale University Press, 2007.

> Another general history, excellent on bringing together the various theatres of war in which the Second Crusade was played out.

Powell, James. *Anatomy of a Crusade, 1213–1221*. Philadelphia: University of Pennsylvania Press, 1986.

> The foundational volume on the Fifth Crusade in Egypt and its military planning.

Riley-Smith, Jonathan. *The Oxford Illustrated History of the Crusades*. Oxford: Oxford University Press, 1995.

> An accessible and useful general history for the novice reader.

—— . *The First Crusade and the Idea of Crusading*. London: Athlone, 1986. Reprinted with a new introduction. London: Continuum, 2009.

> One of Riley-Smith's most important contributions to the mentality of crusading.

Tyerman, Christopher. *The Invention of the Crusades*. Basingstoke: MacMillan, 1998.

> A provocative classic on the terminology of crusading and the development of the category.

Recent Studies

Asbridge, Thomas. "An Experiment in Extremity: The Portrayal of Violence in Robert the Monk's Narrative of the First Crusade." *History: The Journal of the Historical Association* 105, no. 368 (2020): 719–50.

> One of the most recent focussed studies on the idea and representation of crusade violence in an early crusade narrative.

Bachrach, David. *Religion and the Conduct of War c.300–1215*. Woodbridge: Boydell, 2003.

> A very helpful overview of the links between religion and violence in the context of medieval warfare.

Bull, Marcus. *Eyewitness and Crusade Narrative: Perception and Narration in Accounts of the Second, Third and Fourth Crusades*. Woodbridge: Boydell, 2018.

> An important analysis of the ways in which narratives shaped the idea and practice of crusading.

Cobb, Paul. *The Race for Paradise: An Islamic History of the Crusades*. Oxford: Oxford University Press, 2016.

A wonderfully written study of the Islamic history of the crusades and an excellent counterpoint to the many western narratives.

Folda, Jaroslav. *Crusader Art in the Holy Land: From the Third Crusade Until the Fall of Acre*. Cambridge: Cambridge University Press, 2005.

A usefully annotated study of the many material and visual cultures of the crusades, including objects, buildings, paintings, textiles, and more.

Fonnesberg-Schmidt, Iben. *The Popes and the Baltic Crusades, 1147-1254*. Leiden: Brill, 2006.

An excellent study of the crusades against pagans and others in northern Europe.

Gabriele, Matthew. *An Empire of Memory: The Legend of Charlemagne, the Franks, and Jerusalem Before the First Crusade*. Oxford: Oxford University Press, 2011.

A very useful book for thinking about the longer strands of cultural memory that were woven into subsequent histories of crusading.

Gaposchkin, Cecilia. *Invisible Weapons: Liturgy and the Making of Crusade Ideology*. Ithaca: Cornell University Press, 2017.

The most important study of the importance of liturgy in the practice and ideology of crusading.

Hodgson, Natasha. *Women, Crusading and the Holy Land in Historical Narrative*. Woodbridge: Boydell, 2007.

One of the only sustained English-language studies of the place of women in crusading texts.

Lapina, Elizabeth. *Warfare and the Miraculous in the Chronicles of the First Crusade*. University Park: Pennsylvania State University Press, 2015.

A close study of the relationship between violence and miracles in early crusade chronicles.

Mallett, Alex. *Popular Muslim Reactions to the Franks in the Levant, 1097-1291*. Aldershot: Ashgate, 2014.

A very helpful analysis of the impacts of violence on the Muslim populations of the Middle East.

Morton, Nicholas. *The Crusader States and their Neighbours: A Military History, 1099–1187*. Oxford: Oxford University Press, 2020.

> An excellent military history of the twelfth-century crusades, focussing on the many conflicts between all the groups in the region.

Purkis, William. *Crusading Spirituality in the Holy Land and Iberia, c. 1095–c. 1187*. Woodbridge: Boydell, 2008.

> An important analysis of the religious motivations for crusading, including the idea of suffering.

Paterson, Linda. *Singing the Crusades: French and Occitan Lyric Responses to the Crusading Movement, 1137–1336*. Cambridge: Brewer, 2018.

> A wonderful study of the songs from southern France that shaped and reflected ideas of crusading in the region.

Riley-Smith, Jonathan and Susannah Throop. *The Crusades: A History*. 4th ed. London: Bloomsbury, 2022.

> A marvellous update of a classic text which remains a go-to introduction to the crusading movement and its contexts.

Rubenstein, Jay. *Armies of Heaven: The First Crusade and the Quest for Apocalypse*. New York: Basic, 2011.

> An immensely readable work on the apocalyptic ideas underpinning the First Crusade.

Smith, Caroline. *Crusading in the Age of Joinville*. Aldershot: Ashgate, 2006.

> A very accessible history of the crusade of the French king Louis IX.

Smith, Katherine Allen. *The Bible and Crusade Narrative in the Twelfth Century*. Woodbridge: Boydell, 2020.

> A careful and illuminating study of the use of the Bible by chroniclers of the crusades and especially helpful on the use of Scriptural references to justify and promote the crusade.

Spacey, Beth. *The Miraculous and the Writing of Crusade Narrative*. Woodbridge: Boydell, 2020.

> A wide-ranging study of miracles, marvels, and visions during the twelfth-century crusades and the texts that used them.

Spencer, Stephen. *Emotions in a Crusading Context, 1095–1291*. Oxford: Oxford University Press, 2019.

> A pioneering history of emotions during the crusades, and an excellent example of the cultural turn in crusading history.

Throop, Susanna. *Crusading as an Act of Vengeance, 1095–1216*. Farnham: Ashgate, 2011.

> An excellent study of the integration of emotion into the practice of crusading.

——. *The Crusades: An Epitome*. Leeds: Kismet, 2018.

> An extremely helpful short overview of the history of crusading that integrates diverse perspectives very effectively.

Recent Collections

Bird, Jessalynn, ed. *The Papacy, Crusade, and Christian-Muslim Relations: Essays in Memory of James M. Powell*. Amsterdam: University of Amsterdam Press, 2018.

> A diverse set of essays in memory of an exceptional historian. Essays on thirteenth-century preaching, papal directives, and memory.

Buck, Andrew and Thomas W. Smith, eds. *Remembering the Crusades in Medieval Texts and Songs*. Cardiff: University of Wales Press, 2019.

> An excellent set of essays by some of the rising stars of modern crusades studies, dealing with a wide range of crusade sources.

Bull, Marcus and Damien Kempf, eds. *Writing the Early Crusades: Text, Transmission and Memory*. Woodbridge: Boydell, 2014.

> An important collection on the contemporary historical writing on the First Crusade with essays on Latin and Greek texts. See especially Laura Ashe's essay on the idea of knighthood in English and French writing.

Cassidy-Welch, Megan, ed. *Remembering the Crusades and Crusading*. London: Routledge, 2017.

> A collection aimed at considering the sources and historiographies of crusading in a range of contexts from monastic, Jewish, and family memories to Greek, Latvian, and Iberian memories of crusading.

Cassidy-Welch, Megan and Anne E. Lester, eds. "Crusades and Memory." Special issue, *The Journal of Medieval History* 40, no. 3 (2014).

> A collection of articles on the importance of methodologies drawn from memory studies in exploring the history and representation of crusading over time.

Hodgson, Natasha, Katherine Lewis and Matthew Mesley, eds. *Crusading and Masculinities*. Abingdon: Routledge, 2019.

> The first collection to consider how ideas of masculinity informed the practice and idea of crusading, including essays on adolescents, ideas of correct behaviour toward women and representations of gender in various texts. See especially Susan Edgington's essay on "Emasculating the enemy."

Lapina, Elizabeth and Nicholas Morton, eds. *The Uses of the Bible in Crusader Sources*. Leiden: Brill, 2017.

> An excellent collection of essays dealing with the biblical imagery and exegetical interpretations underpinning crusade. See especially Uri Shachar's essay on biblical ideas of sacred space and how these were used to justify violence against Jews in 1096.

Purkis, William J., ed. "Material Religion in the Crusading World." Special issue, *Material Religion* 14, no. 4 (2018).

> A very insightful collection on bodies, places, and things associated with crusading across the eleventh-fifteenth centuries, and an argument for the crusading movement being a "material religion."

Other Resources

Bird, Jessalynn, Edward Peters, and James M. Powell, eds. *Crusade and Christendom: Annotated Documents in Translation from Innocent III to the Fall of Acre, 1187–1291*. Philadelphia: University of Pennsylvania Press, 2013.

Crusades journal. Published by Routledge.

> Contains the latest specialized research on all aspects of crusading and post-crusading history.

Useful websites include

The French of Outremer website.

> A useful collection of sources and thematic essays together with a documentary database. https://frenchofoutremer.ace.fordham.edu.

Regesta Regni Hierosolymitani Database.

> A useful calendar of charters, documents and letters composed in the Latin kingdoms of Jerusalem between 1098 and 1291. http://crusades-regesta.com.

Printed in the United States
by Baker & Taylor Publisher Services